William Shakespeare (bapt. 26 April 1564 – 23 April 1616) was an English poet, playwright and actor, widely regarded as the greatest writer in the English language and the world's greatest dramatist. He is often called England's national poet and the "Bard of Avon". His extant works, including collaborations, consist of approximately 39 plays, 154 sonnets, two long narrative poems, and a few other verses, some of uncertain authorship. His plays have been translated into every major living language and are performed more often than those of any other playwright. Shakespeare was born and raised in Stratford-upon-Avon, Warwickshire. At the age of 18, he married Anne Hathaway, with whom he had three children: Susanna and twins Hamnet and Judith. Sometime between 1585 and 1592, he began a successful career in London as an actor, writer, and part-owner of a playing company called the Lord Chamberlain's Men, later known as the King's Men. At age 49 (around 1613), he appears to have retired to Stratford, where he died three years later. (Source: Wikipedia)

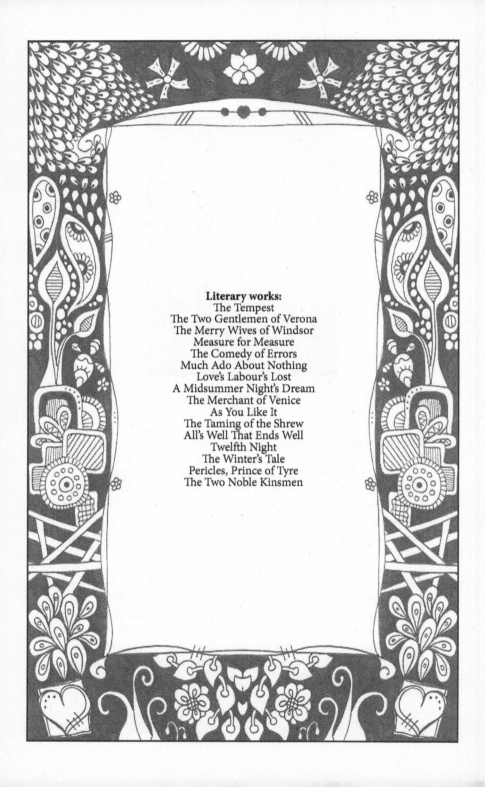

Literary works:
The Tempest
The Two Gentlemen of Verona
The Merry Wives of Windsor
Measure for Measure
The Comedy of Errors
Much Ado About Nothing
Love's Labour's Lost
A Midsummer Night's Dream
The Merchant of Venice
As You Like It
The Taming of the Shrew
All's Well That Ends Well
Twelfth Night
The Winter's Tale
Pericles, Prince of Tyre
The Two Noble Kinsmen

THRONE CLASSICS

THE TWO NOBLE
KINSMEN
William Shakespeare

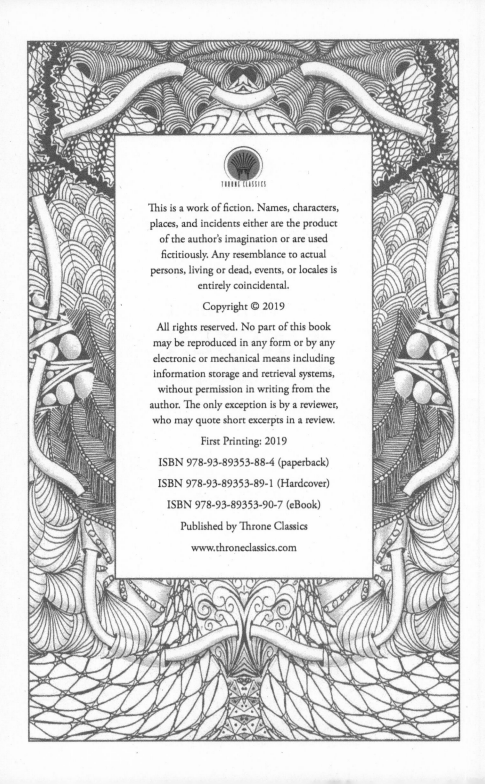

Copyright © 2019

First Printing: 2019

ISBN 978-93-89353-88-4 (paperback)

ISBN 978-93-89353-89-1 (Hardcover)

ISBN 978-93-89353-90-7 (eBook)

Published by Throne Classics

www.throneclassics.com

Contents

THE TWO NOBLE KINSMEN

The Persons represented in the Play.

Hymen,

Theseus,

Hippolita, Bride to Theseus

Emelia, Sister to Theseus

[Emelia's Woman],

Nymphs,

Three Queens,

Three valiant Knights,

Palamon, and

Arcite, The two Noble Kinsmen, in love with fair Emelia

[Valerius],

Perithous,

[A Herald],

[A Gentleman],

[A Messenger],

[A Servant],

[Wooer],

[Keeper],

Jaylor,

His Daughter, in love with Palamon

[His brother],

[A Doctor],

[4] Countreymen,

[2 Friends of the Jaylor],

[3 Knights],

[Nel, and other]

Wenches,

A Taborer,

Gerrold, A Schoolmaster.)

PROLOGUE.

[Florish.]

New Playes, and Maydenheads, are neare a kin,

Much follow'd both, for both much mony g'yn,

If they stand sound, and well: And a good Play

(Whose modest Sceanes blush on his marriage day,

And shake to loose his honour) is like hir

That after holy Tye and first nights stir

Yet still is Modestie, and still retaines

More of the maid to sight, than Husbands paines;

We pray our Play may be so; For I am sure

It has a noble Breeder, and a pure,

A learned, and a Poet never went

More famous yet twixt Po and silver Trent:

Chaucer (of all admir'd) the Story gives,

There constant to Eternity it lives.

If we let fall the Noblenesse of this,

And the first sound this child heare, be a hisse,

How will it shake the bones of that good man,

And make him cry from under ground, 'O fan

From me the witles chaffe of such a wrighter

That blastes my Bayes, and my fam'd workes makes lighter

Then Robin Hood!' This is the feare we bring;

For to say Truth, it were an endlesse thing,

And too ambitious, to aspire to him,

Weake as we are, and almost breathlesse swim

In this deepe water. Do but you hold out

Your helping hands, and we shall take about,

And something doe to save us: You shall heare

Sceanes, though below his Art, may yet appeare

Worth two houres travell. To his bones sweet sleepe:

Content to you. If this play doe not keepe

A little dull time from us, we perceave

Our losses fall so thicke, we must needs leave.

[Florish.]

ACT I

SCENE 1. (Athens. Before a temple.)

[Enter Hymen with a Torch burning: a Boy, in a white Robe before singing, and strewing Flowres: After Hymen, a Nimph, encompast in her Tresses, bearing a wheaten Garland. Then Theseus betweene two other Nimphs with wheaten Chaplets on their heades. Then Hipolita the Bride, lead by Pirithous, and another holding a Garland over her head (her Tresses likewise hanging.) After her Emilia holding up her Traine. (Artesius and Attendants.)]

The Song, [Musike.]

Roses their sharpe spines being gon,

Not royall in their smels alone,

But in their hew.

Maiden Pinckes, of odour faint,

Dazies smel-lesse, yet most quaint

And sweet Time true.

Prim-rose first borne child of Ver,

Merry Spring times Herbinger,

With her bels dimme.

Oxlips, in their Cradles growing,

Mary-golds, on death beds blowing,

Larkes-heeles trymme.

All deere natures children sweete,

Ly fore Bride and Bridegroomes feete, [Strew Flowers.]

Blessing their sence.

Not an angle of the aire,

Bird melodious, or bird faire,

Is absent hence.

The Crow, the slaundrous Cuckoe, nor

The boding Raven, nor Chough hore

Nor chattring Pie,

May on our Bridehouse pearch or sing,

Or with them any discord bring,

But from it fly.

[Enter 3. Queenes in Blacke, with vailes staind, with imperiall Crownes. The 1. Queene fals downe at the foote of Theseus; The 2. fals downe at the foote of Hypolita. The 3. before Emilia.]

1. QUEEN.

For pitties sake and true gentilities,

Heare, and respect me.

2. QUEEN.

For your Mothers sake,

And as you wish your womb may thrive with faire ones,

Heare and respect me.

3. QUEEN

Now for the love of him whom Iove hath markd

The honour of your Bed, and for the sake

Of cleere virginity, be Advocate

For us, and our distresses. This good deede

Shall raze you out o'th Booke of Trespasses

All you are set downe there.

THESEUS.

Sad Lady, rise.

HIPPOLITA.

Stand up.

EMILIA.

No knees to me.

What woman I may steed that is distrest,

Does bind me to her.

THESEUS.

What's your request? Deliver you for all.

1. QUEEN.

We are 3. Queenes, whose Soveraignes fel before

The wrath of cruell Creon; who endured

The Beakes of Ravens, Tallents of the Kights,

And pecks of Crowes, in the fowle feilds of Thebs.

He will not suffer us to burne their bones,

To urne their ashes, nor to take th' offence

Of mortall loathsomenes from the blest eye

Of holy Phoebus, but infects the windes

With stench of our slaine Lords. O pitty, Duke:

Thou purger of the earth, draw thy feard Sword

That does good turnes to'th world; give us the Bones

Of our dead Kings, that we may Chappell them;

And of thy boundles goodnes take some note

That for our crowned heades we have no roofe,

Save this which is the Lyons, and the Beares,

And vault to every thing.

THESEUS.

Pray you, kneele not:

I was transported with your Speech, and suffer'd

Your knees to wrong themselves; I have heard the fortunes

Of your dead Lords, which gives me such lamenting

As wakes my vengeance, and revenge for'em,

King Capaneus was your Lord: the day

That he should marry you, at such a season,

As now it is with me, I met your Groome,

By Marsis Altar; you were that time faire,

Not Iunos Mantle fairer then your Tresses,

Nor in more bounty spread her. Your wheaten wreathe

Was then nor threashd, nor blasted; Fortune at you

Dimpled her Cheeke with smiles: Hercules our kinesman

(Then weaker than your eies) laide by his Club,

He tumbled downe upon his Nemean hide

And swore his sinews thawd: O greife, and time,

Fearefull consumers, you will all devoure.

1. QUEEN.

O, I hope some God,

Some God hath put his mercy in your manhood

Whereto heel infuse powre, and presse you forth

Our undertaker.

THESEUS.

O no knees, none, Widdow,

Vnto the Helmeted Belona use them,

And pray for me your Souldier.

Troubled I am. [turnes away.]

2. QUEEN.

Honoured Hypolita,

Most dreaded Amazonian, that hast slaine

The Sith-tuskd Bore; that with thy Arme as strong

As it is white, wast neere to make the male

To thy Sex captive, but that this thy Lord,

Borne to uphold Creation in that honour

First nature stilde it in, shrunke thee into

The bownd thou wast ore-flowing, at once subduing

Thy force, and thy affection: Soldiresse

That equally canst poize sternenes with pitty,

Whom now I know hast much more power on him

Then ever he had on thee, who ow'st his strength

And his Love too, who is a Servant for

The Tenour of thy Speech: Deere Glasse of Ladies,

Bid him that we, whom flaming war doth scortch,

Vnder the shaddow of his Sword may coole us:

Require him he advance it ore our heades;

Speak't in a womans key: like such a woman

As any of us three; weepe ere you faile;

Lend us a knee;

But touch the ground for us no longer time

Then a Doves motion, when the head's pluckt off:

Tell him if he i'th blood cizd field lay swolne,

Showing the Sun his Teeth, grinning at the Moone,

What you would doe.

HIPPOLITA.

Poore Lady, say no more:

I had as leife trace this good action with you

As that whereto I am going, and never yet

Went I so willing way. My Lord is taken

Hart deepe with your distresse: Let him consider:

Ile speake anon.

3. QUEEN.

O my petition was [kneele to Emilia.]

Set downe in yce, which by hot greefe uncandied

Melts into drops, so sorrow, wanting forme,

Is prest with deeper matter.

EMILIA.

Pray stand up,

Your greefe is written in your cheeke.

3. QUEEN.

O woe,

You cannot reade it there, there through my teares—

Like wrinckled peobles in a glassie streame

You may behold 'em. Lady, Lady, alacke,

He that will all the Treasure know o'th earth

Must know the Center too; he that will fish

For my least minnow, let him lead his line

To catch one at my heart. O pardon me:

Extremity, that sharpens sundry wits,

Makes me a Foole.

EMILIA.

Pray you say nothing, pray you:

Who cannot feele nor see the raine, being in't,

Knowes neither wet nor dry: if that you were

The ground-peece of some Painter, I would buy you

T'instruct me gainst a Capitall greefe indeed—

Such heart peirc'd demonstration; but, alas,

Being a naturall Sifter of our Sex

Your sorrow beates so ardently upon me,

That it shall make a counter reflect gainst

My Brothers heart, and warme it to some pitty,

Though it were made of stone: pray, have good comfort.

THESEUS.

Forward to'th Temple, leave not out a Iot

O'th sacred Ceremony.

1. QUEEN.

O, This Celebration

Will long last, and be more costly then

Your Suppliants war: Remember that your Fame

Knowles in the eare o'th world: what you doe quickly

Is not done rashly; your first thought is more

Then others laboured meditance: your premeditating

More then their actions: But, oh Iove! your actions,

Soone as they mooves, as Asprayes doe the fish,

Subdue before they touch: thinke, deere Duke, thinke

What beds our slaine Kings have.

2. QUEEN.

What greifes our beds,

That our deere Lords have none.

3. QUEEN.

None fit for 'th dead:

Those that with Cordes, Knives, drams precipitance,

Weary of this worlds light, have to themselves

Beene deathes most horrid Agents, humaine grace

Affords them dust and shaddow.

1. QUEEN.

But our Lords

Ly blistring fore the visitating Sunne,

And were good Kings, when living.

THESEUS.

It is true, and I will give you comfort,

To give your dead Lords graves: the which to doe,

Must make some worke with Creon.

1. QUEEN.

And that worke presents it selfe to'th doing:

Now twill take forme, the heates are gone to morrow.

Then, booteles toyle must recompence it selfe

With it's owne sweat; Now he's secure,

Not dreames we stand before your puissance

Wrinching our holy begging in our eyes

To make petition cleere.

2. QUEEN.

Now you may take him, drunke with his victory.

3. QUEEN.

And his Army full of Bread, and sloth.

THESEUS.

Artesius, that best knowest

How to draw out fit to this enterprise

The prim'st for this proceeding, and the number

To carry such a businesse, forth and levy

Our worthiest Instruments, whilst we despatch

This grand act of our life, this daring deede

Of Fate in wedlocke.

1. QUEEN.

Dowagers, take hands;

Let us be Widdowes to our woes: delay

Commends us to a famishing hope.

ALL.

Farewell.

2. QUEEN.

We come unseasonably: But when could greefe

Cull forth, as unpanged judgement can, fit'st time

For best solicitation.

THESEUS.

Why, good Ladies,

This is a service, whereto I am going,

Greater then any was; it more imports me

Then all the actions that I have foregone,

Or futurely can cope.

1. QUEEN.

The more proclaiming

Our suit shall be neglected: when her Armes

Able to locke Iove from a Synod, shall

By warranting Moone-light corslet thee, oh, when

Her twyning Cherries shall their sweetnes fall

Vpon thy tastefull lips, what wilt thou thinke

Of rotten Kings or blubberd Queenes, what care

For what thou feelst not? what thou feelst being able

To make Mars spurne his Drom. O, if thou couch

But one night with her, every howre in't will

Take hostage of thee for a hundred, and

Thou shalt remember nothing more then what

That Banket bids thee too.

HIPPOLITA.

Though much unlike [Kneeling.]

You should be so transported, as much sorry

I should be such a Suitour; yet I thinke,

Did I not by th'abstayning of my joy,

Which breeds a deeper longing, cure their surfeit

That craves a present medcine, I should plucke

All Ladies scandall on me. Therefore, Sir,

As I shall here make tryall of my prayres,

Either presuming them to have some force,

Or sentencing for ay their vigour dombe:

Prorogue this busines we are going about, and hang

Your Sheild afore your Heart, about that necke

Which is my ffee, and which I freely lend

To doe these poore Queenes service.

ALL QUEENS.

Oh helpe now,

Our Cause cries for your knee.

EMILIA.

If you grant not [Kneeling.]

My Sister her petition in that force,

With that Celerity and nature, which

Shee makes it in, from henceforth ile not dare

To aske you any thing, nor be so hardy

Ever to take a Husband.

THESEUS.

Pray stand up.

I am entreating of my selfe to doe

That which you kneele to have me. Pyrithous,

Leade on the Bride; get you and pray the Gods

For successe, and returne; omit not any thing

In the pretended Celebration. Queenes,

Follow your Soldier. As before, hence you [to Artesius]

And at the banckes of Aulis meete us with

The forces you can raise, where we shall finde

The moytie of a number, for a busines

More bigger look't. Since that our Theame is haste,

I stamp this kisse upon thy currant lippe;

Sweete, keepe it as my Token. Set you forward,

For I will see you gone.

                              [Exeunt towards the Temple.]

Farewell, my beauteous Sister: Pyrithous,

Keepe the feast full, bate not an howre on't.

PERITHOUS.

Sir,

Ile follow you at heeles; The Feasts solempnity

Shall want till your returne.

THESEUS.

Cosen, I charge you

Boudge not from Athens; We shall be returning

Ere you can end this Feast, of which, I pray you,

Make no abatement; once more, farewell all.

1. QUEEN.

Thus do'st thou still make good the tongue o'th world.

2. QUEEN.

And earnst a Deity equal with Mars.

3. QUEEN.

If not above him, for

Thou being but mortall makest affections bend

To Godlike honours; they themselves, some say,

Grone under such a Mastry.

THESEUS.

As we are men,

Thus should we doe; being sensually subdude,

We loose our humane tytle. Good cheere, Ladies. [Florish.]

Now turne we towards your Comforts.

[Exeunt.]

SCENE 2. (Thebs).

[Enter Palamon, and Arcite.]

ARCITE.

Deere Palamon, deerer in love then Blood

And our prime Cosen, yet unhardned in

The Crimes of nature; Let us leave the Citty

Thebs, and the temptings in't, before we further

Sully our glosse of youth:

And here to keepe in abstinence we shame

As in Incontinence; for not to swim

I'th aide o'th Current were almost to sincke,

At least to frustrate striving, and to follow

The common Streame, twold bring us to an Edy

Where we should turne or drowne; if labour through,

Our gaine but life, and weakenes.

PALAMON.

Your advice

Is cride up with example: what strange ruins

Since first we went to Schoole, may we perceive

Walking in Thebs? Skars, and bare weedes

The gaine o'th Martialist, who did propound

To his bold ends honour, and golden Ingots,

Which though he won, he had not, and now flurted

By peace for whom he fought: who then shall offer

To Marsis so scornd Altar? I doe bleede

When such I meete, and wish great Iuno would

Resume her ancient fit of Ielouzie

To get the Soldier worke, that peace might purge

For her repletion, and retaine anew

Her charitable heart now hard, and harsher

Then strife or war could be.

ARCITE.

Are you not out?

Meete you no ruine but the Soldier in

The Cranckes and turnes of Thebs? you did begin

As if you met decaies of many kindes:

Perceive you none, that doe arowse your pitty

But th'un-considerd Soldier?

PALAMON.

Yes, I pitty

Decaies where ere I finde them, but such most

That, sweating in an honourable Toyle,

Are paide with yce to coole 'em.

ARCITE.

Tis not this

I did begin to speake of: This is vertue

Of no respect in Thebs; I spake of Thebs

How dangerous if we will keepe our Honours,

It is for our resyding, where every evill

Hath a good cullor; where eve'ry seeming good's

A certaine evill, where not to be ev'n Iumpe

As they are, here were to be strangers, and

Such things to be, meere Monsters.

PALAMON.

Tis in our power,

(Vnlesse we feare that Apes can Tutor's) to

Be Masters of our manners: what neede I

Affect anothers gate, which is not catching

Where there is faith, or to be fond upon

Anothers way of speech, when by mine owne

I may be reasonably conceiv'd; sav'd too,

Speaking it truly? why am I bound

By any generous bond to follow him

Followes his Taylor, haply so long untill

The follow'd make pursuit? or let me know,

Why mine owne Barber is unblest, with him

My poore Chinne too, for tis not Cizard iust

To such a Favorites glasse: What Cannon is there

That does command my Rapier from my hip

To dangle't in my hand, or to go tip toe

Before the streete be foule? Either I am

The fore-horse in the Teame, or I am none

That draw i'th sequent trace: these poore sleight sores

Neede not a plantin; That which rips my bosome

Almost to'th heart's—

ARCITE.

Our Vncle Creon.

PALAMON.

He,

A most unbounded Tyrant, whose successes

Makes heaven unfeard, and villany assured

Beyond its power there's nothing, almost puts

Faith in a feavour, and deifies alone

Voluble chance; who onely attributes

The faculties of other Instruments

To his owne Nerves and act; Commands men service,

And what they winne in't, boot and glory; on(e)

That feares not to do harm; good, dares not; Let

The blood of mine that's sibbe to him be suckt

From me with Leeches; Let them breake and fall

Off me with that corruption.

ARCITE.

Cleere spirited Cozen,

Lets leave his Court, that we may nothing share

Of his lowd infamy: for our milke

Will relish of the pasture, and we must

Be vile or disobedient, not his kinesmen

In blood, unlesse in quality.

PALAMON.

Nothing truer:

I thinke the Ecchoes of his shames have dea'ft

The eares of heav'nly Iustice: widdows cryes

Descend againe into their throates, and have not

[enter Valerius.]

Due audience of the Gods.—Valerius!

VALERIUS.

The King cals for you; yet be leaden footed,

Till his great rage be off him. Phebus, when

He broke his whipstocke and exclaimd against

The Horses of the Sun, but whisperd too

The lowdenesse of his Fury.

PALAMON.

Small windes shake him:

But whats the matter?

VALERIUS.

Theseus (who where he threates appals,) hath sent

Deadly defyance to him, and pronounces

Ruine to Thebs; who is at hand to seale

The promise of his wrath.

ARCITE.

Let him approach;

But that we feare the Gods in him, he brings not

A jot of terrour to us; Yet what man

Thirds his owne worth (the case is each of ours)

When that his actions dregd with minde assurd

Tis bad he goes about?

PALAMON.

Leave that unreasond.

Our services stand now for Thebs, not Creon,

Yet to be neutrall to him were dishonour;

Rebellious to oppose: therefore we must

With him stand to the mercy of our Fate,

Who hath bounded our last minute.

ARCITE.

So we must.

Ist sed this warres a foote? or it shall be,

On faile of some condition?

VALERIUS.

Tis in motion

The intelligence of state came in the instant

With the defier.

PALAMON.

Lets to the king, who, were he

A quarter carrier of that honour which

His Enemy come in, the blood we venture

Should be as for our health, which were not spent,

Rather laide out for purchase: but, alas,

Our hands advanc'd before our hearts, what will

The fall o'th stroke doe damage?

ARCITE.

Let th'event,

That never erring Arbitratour, tell us

When we know all our selves, and let us follow

The becking of our chance.

[Exeunt.]

SCENE 3. (Before the gates of Athens.)

[Enter Pirithous, Hipolita, Emilia.]

PERITHOUS.

No further.

HIPPOLITA.

Sir, farewell; repeat my wishes

To our great Lord, of whose succes I dare not

Make any timerous question; yet I wish him

Exces and overflow of power, and't might be,

To dure ill-dealing fortune: speede to him,

Store never hurtes good Gouernours.

PERITHOUS.

Though I know

His Ocean needes not my poore drops, yet they

Must yeild their tribute there. My precious Maide,

Those best affections, that the heavens infuse

In their best temperd peices, keepe enthroand

In your deare heart.

EMILIA.

Thanckes, Sir. Remember me

To our all royall Brother, for whose speede

The great Bellona ile sollicite; and

Since in our terrene State petitions are not

Without giftes understood, Ile offer to her

What I shall be advised she likes: our hearts

Are in his Army, in his Tent.

HIPPOLITA.

In's bosome:

We have bin Soldiers, and wee cannot weepe

When our Friends don their helmes, or put to sea,

Or tell of Babes broachd on the Launce, or women

That have sod their Infants in (and after eate them)

The brine, they wept at killing 'em; Then if

You stay to see of us such Spincsters, we

Should hold you here for ever.

PERITHOUS.

Peace be to you,

As I pursue this war, which shall be then

Beyond further requiring.

[Exit Pir.]

EMILIA.

How his longing

Followes his Friend! since his depart, his sportes

Though craving seriousnes, and skill, past slightly

His careles execution, where nor gaine

35

Made him regard, or losse consider; but

Playing one busines in his hand, another

Directing in his head, his minde, nurse equall

To these so diffring Twyns—have you observ'd him,

Since our great Lord departed?

HIPPOLITA.

With much labour,

And I did love him fort: they two have Cabind

In many as dangerous, as poore a Corner,

Perill and want contending; they have skift

Torrents whose roring tyranny and power

I'th least of these was dreadfull, and they have

Fought out together, where Deaths-selfe was lodgd,

Yet fate hath brought them off: Their knot of love,

Tide, weau'd, intangled, with so true, so long,

And with a finger of so deepe a cunning,

May be outworne, never undone. I thinke

Theseus cannot be umpire to himselfe,

Cleaving his conscience into twaine and doing

Each side like Iustice, which he loves best.

EMILIA.

Doubtlesse

There is a best, and reason has no manners

To say it is not you: I was acquainted

Once with a time, when I enjoyd a Play-fellow;

You were at wars, when she the grave enrichd,

Who made too proud the Bed, tooke leave o th Moone

(Which then lookt pale at parting) when our count

Was each eleven.

HIPPOLITA.

Twas Flaui(n)a.

EMILIA.

Yes.

You talke of Pirithous and Theseus love;

Theirs has more ground, is more maturely seasond,

More buckled with strong Iudgement and their needes

The one of th'other may be said to water [2. Hearses ready

with Palamon: and Arcite: the 3. Queenes. Theseus: and his

Lordes ready.]

Their intertangled rootes of love; but I

And shee I sigh and spoke of were things innocent,

Lou'd for we did, and like the Elements

That know not what, nor why, yet doe effect

Rare issues by their operance, our soules

Did so to one another; what she lik'd,

Was then of me approov'd, what not, condemd,

No more arraignment; the flowre that I would plucke

And put betweene my breasts (then but beginning

To swell about the blossome) oh, she would long

Till shee had such another, and commit it

To the like innocent Cradle, where Phenix like

They dide in perfume: on my head no toy

But was her patterne; her affections (pretty,

Though, happely, her careles were) I followed

For my most serious decking; had mine eare

Stolne some new aire, or at adventure humd on

From musicall Coynadge, why it was a note

Whereon her spirits would sojourne (rather dwell on)

And sing it in her slumbers. This rehearsall

(Which ev'ry innocent wots well comes in

Like old importments bastard) has this end,

That the true love tweene Mayde, and mayde, may be

More then in sex idividuall.

HIPPOLITA.

Y'are out of breath

And this high speeded pace, is but to say

That you shall never like the Maide Flavina

Love any that's calld Man.

EMILIA.

I am sure I shall not.

HIPPOLITA.

Now, alacke, weake Sister,

I must no more beleeve thee in this point

(Though in't I know thou dost beleeve thy selfe,)

Then I will trust a sickely appetite,

That loathes even as it longs; but, sure, my Sister,

If I were ripe for your perswasion, you

Have saide enough to shake me from the Arme

Of the all noble Theseus, for whose fortunes

I will now in, and kneele with great assurance,

That we, more then his Pirothous, possesse

The high throne in his heart.

EMILIA.

I am not

Against your faith; yet I continew mine.

[Exeunt. Cornets.]

SCENE 4. (A field before Thebes. Dead bodies lying on the ground.)

[A Battaile strooke within: Then a Retrait: Florish. Then Enter Theseus (victor), (Herald and Attendants:) the three Queenes meete him, and fall on their faces before him.]

1. QUEEN.

To thee no starre be darke.

2. QUEEN.

Both heaven and earth

Friend thee for ever.

3. QUEEN.

All the good that may

Be wishd upon thy head, I cry Amen too't.

THESEUS.

Th'imparciall Gods, who from the mounted heavens

View us their mortall Heard, behold who erre,

And in their time chastice: goe and finde out

The bones of your dead Lords, and honour them

With treble Ceremonie; rather then a gap

Should be in their deere rights, we would supply't.

But those we will depute, which shall invest

You in your dignities, and even each thing

Our hast does leave imperfect: So, adiew,

And heavens good eyes looke on you. What are those?

[Exeunt Queenes.]

HERALD.

Men of great quality, as may be judgd

By their appointment; Sone of Thebs have told's

They are Sisters children, Nephewes to the King.

THESEUS.

By'th Helme of Mars, I saw them in the war,

Like to a paire of Lions, smeard with prey,

Make lanes in troopes agast. I fixt my note

Constantly on them; for they were a marke

Worth a god's view: what prisoner was't that told me

When I enquired their names?

HERALD.

Wi'leave, they'r called Arcite and Palamon.

THESEUS.

Tis right: those, those. They are not dead?

HERALD.

Nor in a state of life: had they bin taken,

When their last hurts were given, twas possible [3. Hearses ready.]

They might have bin recovered; Yet they breathe

And haue the name of men.

THESEUS.

Then like men use 'em.

The very lees of such (millions of rates)

Exceede the wine of others: all our Surgions

Convent in their behoofe; our richest balmes

Rather then niggard, waft: their lives concerne us

Much more then Thebs is worth: rather then have 'em

Freed of this plight, and in their morning state

(Sound and at liberty) I would 'em dead;

But forty thousand fold we had rather have 'em

Prisoners to us then death. Beare 'em speedily

From our kinde aire, to them unkinde, and minister

What man to man may doe—for our sake more,

Since I have knowne frights, fury, friends beheastes,

Loves provocations, zeale, a mistris Taske,

Desire of liberty, a feavour, madnes,

Hath set a marke which nature could not reach too

Without some imposition: sicknes in will

Or wrastling strength in reason. For our Love

And great Appollos mercy, all our best

Their best skill tender. Leade into the Citty,

Where having bound things scatterd, we will post [Florish.]

To Athens for(e) our Army

[Exeunt. Musicke.]

SCENE 5. (Another part of the same.)

[Enter the Queenes with the Hearses of their Knightes, in a Funerall Solempnity, &c.]

Vrnes and odours bring away,

Vapours, sighes, darken the day;

Our dole more deadly lookes than dying;

Balmes, and Gummes, and heavy cheeres,

Sacred vials fill'd with teares,

And clamors through the wild ayre flying.

Come all sad and solempne Showes,

That are quick-eyd pleasures foes;

We convent nought else but woes.

We convent, &c.

3. QUEEN.

This funeral path brings to your housholds grave:

Ioy ceaze on you againe: peace sleepe with him.

2. QUEEN.

And this to yours.

1. QUEEN.

Yours this way: Heavens lend

A thousand differing waies to one sure end.

3. QUEEN.

This world's a Citty full of straying Streetes, And Death's the market place, where each one meetes.

[Exeunt severally.]

ACT II

SCENE 1. (Athens. A garden, with a prison in the background.)

[Enter Iailor, and Wooer.]

IAILOR.

I may depart with little, while I live; some thing I may cast to you, not much: Alas, the Prison I keepe, though it be for great ones, yet they seldome come; Before one Salmon, you shall take a number of Minnowes. I am given out to be better lyn'd then it can appeare to me report is a true Speaker: I would I were really that I am deliverd to be. Marry, what I have (be it what it will) I will assure upon my daughter at the day of my death.

WOOER.

Sir, I demaund no more then your owne offer, and I will estate

your

Daughter in what I have promised.

IAILOR.

Wel, we will talke more of this, when the solemnity is past. But have you a full promise of her? When that shall be seene, I tender my consent.

[Enter Daughter.]

WOOER.

I have Sir; here shee comes.

IAILOR.

Your Friend and I have chanced to name you here, upon the old busines: But no more of that now; so soone as the Court hurry is over, we will have an end of it: I'th meane time looke tenderly to the two Prisoners. I can tell you they are princes.

DAUGHTER.

These strewings are for their Chamber; tis pitty they are in prison, and twer pitty they should be out: I doe thinke they have patience to make any adversity asham'd; the prison it selfe is proud of 'em; and they have all the world in their Chamber.

IAILOR.

They are fam'd to be a paire of absolute men.

DAUGHTER.

By my troth, I think Fame but stammers 'em; they stand a greise above the reach of report.

IAILOR.

I heard them reported in the Battaile to be the only doers.

DAUGHTER.

Nay, most likely, for they are noble suffrers; I mervaile how they would have lookd had they beene Victors, that with such a constant Nobility enforce a freedome out of Bondage, making misery their Mirth, and affliction a toy to jest at.

IAILOR.

Doe they so?

DAUGHTER.

It seemes to me they have no more sence of their Captivity, then I of ruling Athens: they eate well, looke merrily, discourse of many things, but nothing of their owne restraint, and disasters: yet sometime a devided sigh, martyrd as 'twer i'th deliverance, will breake from one of them; when the other presently gives it so sweete a rebuke, that I could wish my selfe a Sigh

46

to be so chid, or at least a Sigher to be comforted.

WOOER.

I never saw 'em.

IAILOR.

The Duke himselfe came privately in the night,

[Enter Palamon, and Arcite, above.]

and so did they: what the reason of it is, I know not: Looke, yonder they are! that's Arcite lookes out.

DAUGHTER.

No, Sir, no, that's Palamon: Arcite is the lower of the twaine; you may perceive a part of him.

IAILOR.

Goe too, leave your pointing; they would not make us their object; out of their sight.

DAUGHTER.

It is a holliday to looke on them: Lord, the diffrence of men!

[Exeunt.]

SCENE 2. (The prison)

[Enter Palamon, and Arcite in prison.]

PALAMON.

How doe you, Noble Cosen?

ARCITE.

How doe you, Sir?

PALAMON.

Why strong inough to laugh at misery,

And beare the chance of warre, yet we are prisoners,

I feare, for ever, Cosen.

ARCITE.

I beleeve it,

And to that destiny have patiently

Laide up my houre to come.

PALAMON.

O Cosen Arcite,

Where is Thebs now? where is our noble Country?

Where are our friends, and kindreds? never more

Must we behold those comforts, never see

The hardy youthes strive for the Games of honour

(Hung with the painted favours of their Ladies,

Like tall Ships under saile) then start among'st 'em

And as an Eastwind leave 'en all behinde us,

Like lazy Clowdes, whilst Palamon and Arcite,

Even in the wagging of a wanton leg

Out-stript the peoples praises, won the Garlands,

Ere they have time to wish 'em ours. O never

Shall we two exercise, like Twyns of honour,

Our Armes againe, and feele our fyry horses

Like proud Seas under us: our good Swords now

(Better the red-eyd god of war nev'r wore)

Ravishd our sides, like age must run to rust,

And decke the Temples of those gods that hate us:

These hands shall never draw'em out like lightning,

To blast whole Armies more.

ARCITE.

No, Palamon,

Those hopes are Prisoners with us; here we are

And here the graces of our youthes must wither

Like a too-timely Spring; here age must finde us,

And, which is heaviest, Palamon, unmarried;

The sweete embraces of a loving wife,

Loden with kisses, armd with thousand Cupids

Shall never claspe our neckes, no issue know us,

No figures of our selves shall we ev'r see,

To glad our age, and like young Eagles teach 'em

Boldly to gaze against bright armes, and say:

'Remember what your fathers were, and conquer.'

The faire-eyd Maides, shall weepe our Banishments,

And in their Songs, curse ever-blinded fortune,

Till shee for shame see what a wrong she has done

To youth and nature. This is all our world;

We shall know nothing here but one another,

Heare nothing but the Clocke that tels our woes.

The Vine shall grow, but we shall never see it:

Sommer shall come, and with her all delights;

But dead-cold winter must inhabite here still.

PALAMON.

Tis too true, Arcite. To our Theban houndes,

That shooke the aged Forrest with their ecchoes,

No more now must we halloa, no more shake

Our pointed Iavelyns, whilst the angry Swine

Flyes like a parthian quiver from our rages,

Strucke with our well-steeld Darts: All valiant uses

(The foode, and nourishment of noble mindes,)

In us two here shall perish; we shall die

(Which is the curse of honour) lastly

Children of greife, and Ignorance.

ARCITE.

Yet, Cosen,

Even from the bottom of these miseries,

From all that fortune can inflict upon us,

I see two comforts rysing, two meere blessings,

If the gods please: to hold here a brave patience,

And the enjoying of our greefes together.

Whilst Palamon is with me, let me perish

If I thinke this our prison.

PALAMON.

Certeinly,

Tis a maine goodnes, Cosen, that our fortunes

Were twyn'd together; tis most true, two soules

Put in two noble Bodies—let 'em suffer

The gaule of hazard, so they grow together—

Will never sincke; they must not, say they could:

A willing man dies sleeping, and all's done.

ARCITE.

Shall we make worthy uses of this place

That all men hate so much?

PALAMON.

How, gentle Cosen?

ARCITE.

Let's thinke this prison holy sanctuary,

To keepe us from corruption of worse men.

We are young and yet desire the waies of honour,

That liberty and common Conversation,

The poyson of pure spirits, might like women

Wooe us to wander from. What worthy blessing

Can be but our Imaginations

May make it ours? And heere being thus together,

We are an endles mine to one another;

We are one anothers wife, ever begetting

New birthes of love; we are father, friends, acquaintance;

We are, in one another, Families,

I am your heire, and you are mine: This place

Is our Inheritance, no hard Oppressour

Dare take this from us; here, with a little patience,

We shall live long, and loving: No surfeits seeke us:

The hand of war hurts none here, nor the Seas

Swallow their youth: were we at liberty,

A wife might part us lawfully, or busines;

Quarrels consume us, Envy of ill men

Grave our acquaintance; I might sicken, Cosen,

Where you should never know it, and so perish

Without your noble hand to close mine eies,

Or praiers to the gods: a thousand chaunces,

Were we from hence, would seaver us.

PALAMON.

You have made me

(I thanke you, Cosen Arcite) almost wanton

With my Captivity: what a misery

It is to live abroade, and every where!

Tis like a Beast, me thinkes: I finde the Court here—

I am sure, a more content; and all those pleasures

That wooe the wils of men to vanity,

I see through now, and am sufficient

To tell the world, tis but a gaudy shaddow,

That old Time, as he passes by, takes with him.

What had we bin, old in the Court of Creon,

Where sin is Iustice, lust and ignorance

The vertues of the great ones! Cosen Arcite,

Had not the loving gods found this place for us,

We had died as they doe, ill old men, unwept,

And had their Epitaphes, the peoples Curses:

Shall I say more?

ARCITE.

I would heare you still.

PALAMON.

Ye shall.

Is there record of any two that lov'd

Better then we doe, Arcite?

ARCITE.

Sure, there cannot.

PALAMON.

I doe not thinke it possible our friendship

Should ever leave us.

ARCITE.

Till our deathes it cannot;

[Enter Emilia and her woman (below).]

And after death our spirits shall be led

To those that love eternally. Speake on, Sir.

EMILIA.

This garden has a world of pleasures in't.

What Flowre is this?

WOMAN.

Tis calld Narcissus, Madam.

EMILIA.

That was a faire Boy, certaine, but a foole,

To love himselfe; were there not maides enough?

ARCITE.

Pray forward.

PALAMON.

Yes.

EMILIA.

Or were they all hard hearted?

WOMAN.

They could not be to one so faire.

EMILIA.

Thou wouldst not.

WOMAN.

I thinke I should not, Madam.

EMILIA.

That's a good wench:

But take heede to your kindnes though.

WOMAN.

Why, Madam?

EMILIA.

Men are mad things.

ARCITE.

Will ye goe forward, Cosen?

EMILIA.

Canst not thou worke such flowers in silke, wench?

WOMAN.

Yes.

EMILIA.

Ile have a gowne full of 'em, and of these;

This is a pretty colour, wilt not doe

Rarely upon a Skirt, wench?

WOMAN.

Deinty, Madam.

ARCITE.

Cosen, Cosen, how doe you, Sir? Why, Palamon?

PALAMON.

Never till now I was in prison, Arcite.

ARCITE.

Why whats the matter, Man?

PALAMON.

Behold, and wonder.

By heaven, shee is a Goddesse.

ARCITE.

Ha.

PALAMON.

Doe reverence. She is a Goddesse, Arcite.

EMILIA.

Of all Flowres, me thinkes a Rose is best.

WOMAN.

Why, gentle Madam?

EMILIA.

It is the very Embleme of a Maide.

For when the west wind courts her gently,

How modestly she blowes, and paints the Sun,

With her chaste blushes! When the North comes neere her,

Rude and impatient, then, like Chastity,

Shee lockes her beauties in her bud againe,

And leaves him to base briers.

WOMAN.

Yet, good Madam,

Sometimes her modesty will blow so far

She fals for't: a Mayde,

If shee have any honour, would be loth

To take example by her.

EMILIA.

Thou art wanton.

ARCITE.

She is wondrous faire.

PALAMON.

She is beauty extant.

EMILIA.

The Sun grows high, lets walk in: keep these flowers;

Weele see how neere Art can come neere their colours.

I am wondrous merry hearted, I could laugh now.

WOMAN.

I could lie downe, I am sure.

EMILIA.

And take one with you?

WOMAN.

That's as we bargaine, Madam.

EMILIA.

Well, agree then.

[Exeunt Emilia and woman.]

PALAMON.

What thinke you of this beauty?

ARCITE.

Tis a rare one.

PALAMON.

Is't but a rare one?

ARCITE.

Yes, a matchles beauty.

PALAMON.

Might not a man well lose himselfe and love her?

ARCITE.

I cannot tell what you have done, I have;

Beshrew mine eyes for't: now I feele my Shackles.

PALAMON.

You love her, then?

ARCITE.

Who would not?

PALAMON.

And desire her?

ARCITE.

Before my liberty.

PALAMON.

I saw her first.

ARCITE.

That's nothing.

PALAMON.

But it shall be.

ARCITE.

I saw her too.

PALAMON.

Yes, but you must not love her.

ARCITE.

I will not as you doe, to worship her,

As she is heavenly, and a blessed Goddes;

I love her as a woman, to enjoy her:

So both may love.

PALAMON.

You shall not love at all.

ARCITE.

Not love at all!

Who shall deny me?

PALAMON.

I, that first saw her; I, that tooke possession

First with mine eyes of all those beauties

In her reveald to mankinde: if thou lou'st her,

Or entertain'st a hope to blast my wishes,

Thou art a Traytour, Arcite, and a fellow

False as thy Title to her: friendship, blood,

And all the tyes betweene us I disclaime,

If thou once thinke upon her.

ARCITE.

Yes, I love her,

And if the lives of all my name lay on it,

I must doe so; I love her with my soule:

If that will lose ye, farewell, Palamon;

I say againe, I love, and in loving her maintaine

I am as worthy and as free a lover,

And have as just a title to her beauty

As any Palamon or any living

That is a mans Sonne.

PALAMON.

Have I cald thee friend?

ARCITE.

Yes, and have found me so; why are you mov'd thus?

Let me deale coldly with you: am not I

Part of your blood, part of your soule? you have told me

That I was Palamon, and you were Arcite.

PALAMON.

Yes.

ARCITE.

Am not I liable to those affections,

Those joyes, greifes, angers, feares, my friend shall suffer?

PALAMON.

Ye may be.

ARCITE.

Why, then, would you deale so cunningly,

So strangely, so vnlike a noble kinesman,

To love alone? speake truely: doe you thinke me

Vnworthy of her sight?

PALAMON.

No; but unjust,

If thou pursue that sight.

ARCITE.

Because an other

First sees the Enemy, shall I stand still

And let mine honour downe, and never charge?

PALAMON.

Yes, if he be but one.

ARCITE.

But say that one

Had rather combat me?

PALAMON.

Let that one say so,

And use thy freedome; els if thou pursuest her,

Be as that cursed man that hates his Country,

A branded villaine.

ARCITE.

You are mad.

PALAMON.

I must be,

Till thou art worthy, Arcite; it concernes me,

And in this madnes, if I hazard thee

And take thy life, I deale but truely.

ARCITE.

Fie, Sir,

You play the Childe extreamely: I will love her,

I must, I ought to doe so, and I dare;

And all this justly.

PALAMON.

O that now, that now

Thy false-selfe and thy friend had but this fortune,

To be one howre at liberty, and graspe

Our good Swords in our hands! I would quickly teach thee

What 'twer to filch affection from another:

Thou art baser in it then a Cutpurse;

Put but thy head out of this window more,

And as I have a soule, Ile naile thy life too't.

ARCITE.

Thou dar'st not, foole, thou canst not, thou art feeble.

Put my head out? Ile throw my Body out,

And leape the garden, when I see her next

[Enter Keeper.]

And pitch between her armes to anger thee.

PALAMON.

No more; the keeper's comming; I shall live

To knocke thy braines out with my Shackles.

ARCITE.

Doe.

KEEPER.

By your leave, Gentlemen—

PALAMON.

Now, honest keeper?

KEEPER.

Lord Arcite, you must presently to'th Duke;

The cause I know not yet.

ARCITE.

I am ready, keeper.

KEEPER.

Prince Palamon, I must awhile bereave you

Of your faire Cosens Company.

[Exeunt Arcite, and Keeper.]

PALAMON.

And me too,

Even when you please, of life. Why is he sent for?

It may be he shall marry her; he's goodly,

And like enough the Duke hath taken notice

Both of his blood and body: But his falsehood!

Why should a friend be treacherous? If that

Get him a wife so noble, and so faire,

Let honest men ne're love againe. Once more

I would but see this faire One. Blessed Garden,

And fruite, and flowers more blessed, that still blossom

As her bright eies shine on ye! would I were,

For all the fortune of my life hereafter,

Yon little Tree, yon blooming Apricocke;

How I would spread, and fling my wanton armes

In at her window; I would bring her fruite

Fit for the Gods to feed on: youth and pleasure

Still as she tasted should be doubled on her,

And if she be not heavenly, I would make her

So neere the Gods in nature, they should feare her,

[Enter Keeper.]

And then I am sure she would love me. How now, keeper.

Wher's Arcite?

KEEPER.

Banishd: Prince Pirithous

Obtained his liberty; but never more

Vpon his oth and life must he set foote

Vpon this Kingdome.

PALAMON.

Hees a blessed man!

He shall see Thebs againe, and call to Armes

The bold yong men, that, when he bids 'em charge,

Fall on like fire: Arcite shall have a Fortune,

If he dare make himselfe a worthy Lover,

Yet in the Feild to strike a battle for her;

And if he lose her then, he's a cold Coward;

How bravely may he beare himselfe to win her

If he be noble Arcite—thousand waies.

Were I at liberty, I would doe things

Of such a vertuous greatnes, that this Lady,

This blushing virgine, should take manhood to her

And seeke to ravish me.

KEEPER.

My Lord for you

I have this charge too—

PALAMON.

To discharge my life?

KEEPER.

No, but from this place to remoove your Lordship:

The windowes are too open.

PALAMON.

Devils take 'em,

That are so envious to me! pre'thee kill me.

KEEPER.

And hang for't afterward.

PALAMON.

By this good light,

Had I a sword I would kill thee.

KEEPER.

Why, my Lord?

PALAMON.

Thou bringst such pelting scuruy news continually

Thou art not worthy life. I will not goe.

KEEPER.

Indeede, you must, my Lord.

PALAMON.

May I see the garden?

KEEPER.

Noe.

PALAMON.

Then I am resolud, I will not goe.

KEEPER.

I must constraine you then: and for you are dangerous,

Ile clap more yrons on you.

PALAMON.

Doe, good keeper.

Ile shake 'em so, ye shall not sleepe;

Ile make ye a new Morrisse: must I goe?

KEEPER.

There is no remedy.

PALAMON.

Farewell, kinde window.

May rude winde never hurt thee. O, my Lady,

If ever thou hast felt what sorrow was,

Dreame how I suffer. Come; now bury me.

[Exeunt Palamon, and Keeper.]

SCENE 3. (The country near Athens.

[Enter Arcite.]

ARCITE.

Banishd the kingdome? tis a benefit,

A mercy I must thanke 'em for, but banishd

The free enjoying of that face I die for,

Oh twas a studdied punishment, a death

Beyond Imagination: Such a vengeance

That, were I old and wicked, all my sins

Could never plucke upon me. Palamon,

Thou ha'st the Start now, thou shalt stay and see

Her bright eyes breake each morning gainst thy window,

And let in life into thee; thou shalt feede

Vpon the sweetenes of a noble beauty,

That nature nev'r exceeded, nor nev'r shall:

Good gods! what happines has Palamon!

Twenty to one, hee'le come to speake to her,

And if she be as gentle as she's faire,

I know she's his; he has a Tongue will tame

Tempests, and make the wild Rockes wanton.

Come what can come,

The worst is death; I will not leave the Kingdome.

I know mine owne is but a heape of ruins,

And no redresse there; if I goe, he has her.

I am resolu'd an other shape shall make me,

Or end my fortunes. Either way, I am happy:

Ile see her, and be neere her, or no more.

[Enter 4. Country people, & one with a garlond before them.]

1. COUNTREYMAN

My Masters, ile be there, that's certaine

2. COUNTREYMAN

And Ile be there.

3. COUNTREYMAN

And I.

4. COUNTREYMAN

Why, then, have with ye, Boyes; Tis but a chiding.

Let the plough play to day, ile tick'lt out

Of the Iades tailes to morrow.

1. COUNTREYMAN

I am sure

To have my wife as jealous as a Turkey:

But that's all one; ile goe through, let her mumble.

2. COUNTREYMAN

Clap her aboard to morrow night, and stoa her,

And all's made up againe.

3. COUNTREYMAN

I, doe but put a feskue in her fist, and you shall see her

Take a new lesson out, and be a good wench.

Doe we all hold against the Maying?

4. COUNTREYMAN

Hold? what should aile us?

3. COUNTREYMAN

Arcas will be there.

2. COUNTREYMAN

And Sennois.

And Rycas, and 3. better lads nev'r dancd

Under green Tree. And yee know what wenches: ha?

But will the dainty Domine, the Schoolemaster,

Keep touch, doe you thinke? for he do's all, ye know.

3. COUNTREYMAN

Hee'l eate a hornebooke ere he faile: goe too, the matter's too farre driven betweene him and the Tanners daughter, to let slip now, and she must see the Duke, and she must daunce too.

4. COUNTREYMAN

Shall we be lusty?

2. COUNTREYMAN

All the Boyes in Athens blow wind i'th breech on's, and heere ile be and there ile be, for our Towne, and here againe, and there againe: ha, Boyes, heigh for the weavers.

1. COUNTREYMAN

This must be done i'th woods.

4. COUNTREYMAN

O, pardon me.

2. COUNTREYMAN

By any meanes, our thing of learning saies so:

Where he himselfe will edifie the Duke

Most parlously in our behalfes: hees excellent i'th woods;

Bring him to'th plaines, his learning makes no cry.

3. COUNTREYMAN

Weele see the sports, then; every man to's Tackle:

And, Sweete Companions, lets rehearse by any meanes,

Before the Ladies see us, and doe sweetly,

And God knows what May come on't.

4. COUNTREYMAN

Content; the sports once ended, wee'l performe.

Away, Boyes and hold.

ARCITE.

By your leaves, honest friends: pray you, whither goe you?

4. COUNTREYMAN

Whither? why, what a question's that?

ARCITE.

Yes, tis a question, to me that know not.

3. COUNTREYMAN

To the Games, my Friend.

2. COUNTREYMAN

Where were you bred, you know it not?

ARCITE.

Not farre, Sir,

Are there such Games to day?

1. COUNTREYMAN

Yes, marry, are there:

And such as you neuer saw; The Duke himselfe

Will be in person there.

ARCITE.

What pastimes are they?

2. COUNTREYMAN

Wrastling, and Running.—Tis a pretty Fellow.

3. COUNTREYMAN

Thou wilt not goe along?

ARCITE.

Not yet, Sir.

4. COUNTREYMAN

Well, Sir,

Take your owne time: come, Boyes.

1. COUNTREYMAN

My minde misgives me;

This fellow has a veng'ance tricke o'th hip:

Marke how his Bodi's made for't

2. COUNTREYMAN

Ile be hangd, though,

If he dare venture; hang him, plumb porredge,

He wrastle? he rost eggs! Come, lets be gon, Lads.

[Exeunt.]

ARCITE.

This is an offerd oportunity

I durst not wish for. Well I could have wrestled,

The best men calld it excellent, and run—

Swifter the winde upon a feild of Corne

(Curling the wealthy eares) never flew: Ile venture,

And in some poore disguize be there; who knowes

Whether my browes may not be girt with garlands?

And happines preferre me to a place,

Where I may ever dwell in sight of her. [Exit Arcite.]

SCENE 4. (Athens. A room in the prison.)

[Enter Iailors Daughter alone.]

DAUGHTER.

Why should I love this Gentleman? Tis odds

He never will affect me; I am base,

My Father the meane Keeper of his Prison,

And he a prince: To marry him is hopelesse;

To be his whore is witles. Out upon't,

What pushes are we wenches driven to,

When fifteene once has found us! First, I saw him;

I (seeing) thought he was a goodly man;

He has as much to please a woman in him,

(If he please to bestow it so) as ever

These eyes yet lookt on. Next, I pittied him,

And so would any young wench, o' my Conscience,

That ever dream'd, or vow'd her Maydenhead

To a yong hansom Man; Then I lov'd him,

Extreamely lov'd him, infinitely lov'd him;

And yet he had a Cosen, faire as he too.

But in my heart was Palamon, and there,

Lord, what a coyle he keepes! To heare him

Sing in an evening, what a heaven it is!

And yet his Songs are sad ones. Fairer spoken

Was never Gentleman. When I come in

To bring him water in a morning, first

He bowes his noble body, then salutes me, thus:

'Faire, gentle Mayde, good morrow; may thy goodnes

Get thee a happy husband.' Once he kist me.

I lov'd my lips the better ten daies after.

Would he would doe so ev'ry day! He greives much,

And me as much to see his misery.

What should I doe, to make him know I love him?

For I would faine enjoy him. Say I ventur'd

To set him free? what saies the law then? Thus much

For Law, or kindred! I will doe it,

And this night, or to morrow, he shall love me.

[Exit.]

SCENE 5. (An open place in Athens.)

[Enter Theseus, Hipolita, Pirithous, Emilia: Arcite with a Garland, &c.]

[This short florish of Cornets and Showtes within.]

THESEUS.

You have done worthily; I have not seene,

Since Hercules, a man of tougher synewes;

What ere you are, you run the best, and wrastle,

That these times can allow.

ARCITE.

I am proud to please you.

THESEUS.

What Countrie bred you?

ARCITE.

This; but far off, Prince.

THESEUS.

Are you a Gentleman?

ARCITE.

My father said so;

And to those gentle uses gave me life.

THESEUS.

Are you his heire?

ARCITE.

His yongest, Sir.

THESEUS.

Your Father

Sure is a happy Sire then: what prooves you?

ARCITE.

A little of all noble Quallities:

I could have kept a Hawke, and well have holloa'd

To a deepe crie of Dogges; I dare not praise

My feat in horsemanship, yet they that knew me

Would say it was my best peece: last, and greatest,

I would be thought a Souldier.

THESEUS.

You are perfect.

PERITHOUS.

Vpon my soule, a proper man.

EMILIA.

He is so.

PERITHOUS.

How doe you like him, Ladie?

HIPPOLITA.

I admire him;

I have not seene so yong a man so noble

(If he say true,) of his sort.

EMILIA.

Beleeve,

His mother was a wondrous handsome woman;

His face, me thinkes, goes that way.

HIPPOLITA.

But his Body

And firie minde illustrate a brave Father.

PERITHOUS.

Marke how his vertue, like a hidden Sun,

Breakes through his baser garments.

HIPPOLITA.

Hee's well got, sure.

THESEUS.

What made you seeke this place, Sir?

ARCITE.

Noble Theseus,

To purchase name, and doe my ablest service

To such a well-found wonder as thy worth,

For onely in thy Court, of all the world,

Dwells faire-eyd honor.

PERITHOUS.

All his words are worthy.

THESEUS.

Sir, we are much endebted to your travell,

Nor shall you loose your wish: Perithous,

Dispose of this faire Gentleman.

PERITHOUS.

Thankes, Theseus.

What ere you are y'ar mine, and I shall give you

To a most noble service, to this Lady,

This bright yong Virgin; pray, observe her goodnesse;

You have honourd hir faire birth-day with your vertues,

And as your due y'ar hirs: kisse her faire hand, Sir.

ARCITE.

Sir, y'ar a noble Giver: dearest Bewtie,

Thus let me seale my vowd faith: when your Servant

(Your most unworthie Creature) but offends you,

Command him die, he shall.

EMILIA.

That were too cruell.

If you deserve well, Sir, I shall soone see't:

Y'ar mine, and somewhat better than your rancke

Ile use you.

PERITHOUS.

Ile see you furnish'd, and because you say

You are a horseman, I must needs intreat you

This after noone to ride, but tis a rough one.

ARCITE.

I like him better, Prince, I shall not then

Freeze in my Saddle.

THESEUS.

Sweet, you must be readie,

And you, Emilia, and you, Friend, and all,

To morrow by the Sun, to doe observance

To flowry May, in Dians wood: waite well, Sir,

Vpon your Mistris. Emely, I hope

He shall not goe a foote.

EMILIA.

That were a shame, Sir,

While I have horses: take your choice, and what

You want at any time, let me but know it;

If you serve faithfully, I dare assure you

You'l finde a loving Mistris.

ARCITE.

If I doe not,

Let me finde that my Father ever hated,

Disgrace and blowes.

THESEUS.

Go, leade the way; you have won it:

It shall be so; you shall receave all dues

Fit for the honour you have won; Twer wrong else.

Sister, beshrew my heart, you have a Servant,

That, if I were a woman, would be Master,

But you are wise. [Florish.]

EMILIA.

I hope too wise for that, Sir.

[Exeunt omnes.]

SCENE 6. (Before the prison.)

[Enter Iaylors Daughter alone.]

DAUGHTER.

Let all the Dukes, and all the divells rore,

He is at liberty: I have venturd for him,

And out I have brought him to a little wood

A mile hence. I have sent him, where a Cedar,

Higher than all the rest, spreads like a plane

Fast by a Brooke, and there he shall keepe close,

Till I provide him Fyles and foode, for yet

His yron bracelets are not off. O Love,

What a stout hearted child thou art! My Father

Durst better have indur'd cold yron, than done it:

I love him beyond love and beyond reason,

Or wit, or safetie: I have made him know it.

I care not, I am desperate; If the law

Finde me, and then condemne me for't, some wenches,

Some honest harted Maides, will sing my Dirge,

And tell to memory my death was noble,

Dying almost a Martyr: That way he takes,

I purpose is my way too: Sure he cannot

Be so unmanly, as to leave me here;

If he doe, Maides will not so easily

Trust men againe: And yet he has not thank'd me

For what I have done: no not so much as kist me,

And that (me thinkes) is not so well; nor scarcely

Could I perswade him to become a Freeman,

He made such scruples of the wrong he did

To me, and to my Father. Yet I hope,

When he considers more, this love of mine

Will take more root within him: Let him doe

What he will with me, so he use me kindly;

For use me so he shall, or ile proclaime him,

And to his face, no man. Ile presently

Provide him necessaries, and packe my cloathes up,

And where there is a patch of ground Ile venture,

So hee be with me; By him, like a shadow,

Ile ever dwell; within this houre the whoobub

Will be all ore the prison: I am then

Kissing the man they looke for: farewell, Father;

Get many more such prisoners and such daughters,

And shortly you may keepe your selfe. Now to him!

ACT III

SCENE 1. (A forest near Athens.)

[Cornets in sundry places. Noise and hallowing as people a Maying.]

[Enter Arcite alone.]

ARCITE.

The Duke has lost Hypolita; each tooke

A severall land. This is a solemne Right

They owe bloomd May, and the Athenians pay it

To'th heart of Ceremony. O Queene Emilia,

Fresher then May, sweeter

Then hir gold Buttons on the bowes, or all

Th'enamelld knackes o'th Meade or garden: yea,

We challenge too the bancke of any Nymph

That makes the streame seeme flowers; thou, o Iewell

O'th wood, o'th world, hast likewise blest a place

With thy sole presence: in thy rumination

That I, poore man, might eftsoones come betweene

And chop on some cold thought! thrice blessed chance,

To drop on such a Mistris, expectation

Most giltlesse on't! tell me, O Lady Fortune,

(Next after Emely my Soveraigne) how far

I may be prowd. She takes strong note of me,

Hath made me neere her; and this beuteous Morne

(The prim'st of all the yeare) presents me with

A brace of horses: two such Steeds might well

Be by a paire of Kings backt, in a Field

That their crownes titles tride. Alas, alas,

Poore Cosen Palamon, poore prisoner, thou

So little dream'st upon my fortune, that

Thou thinkst thy selfe the happier thing, to be

So neare Emilia; me thou deem'st at Thebs,

And therein wretched, although free. But if

Thou knew'st my Mistris breathd on me, and that

I ear'd her language, livde in her eye, O Coz,

What passion would enclose thee!

[Enter Palamon as out of a Bush, with his Shackles: bends his fist at Arcite.]

PALAMON.

Traytor kinesman,

Thou shouldst perceive my passion, if these signes

Of prisonment were off me, and this hand

But owner of a Sword: By all othes in one,

I and the iustice of my love would make thee

A confest Traytor. O thou most perfidious

That ever gently lookd; the voydest of honour,

That eu'r bore gentle Token; falsest Cosen

That ever blood made kin, call'st thou hir thine?

Ile prove it in my Shackles, with these hands,

Void of appointment, that thou ly'st, and art

A very theefe in love, a Chaffy Lord,

Nor worth the name of villaine: had I a Sword

And these house clogges away—

ARCITE.

Deere Cosin Palamon—

PALAMON.

Cosoner Arcite, give me language such

As thou hast shewd me feate.

ARCITE.

Not finding in

The circuit of my breast any grosse stuffe

To forme me like your blazon, holds me to

This gentlenesse of answer; tis your passion

That thus mistakes, the which to you being enemy,

Cannot to me be kind: honor, and honestie

I cherish, and depend on, how so ev'r

You skip them in me, and with them, faire Coz,

Ile maintaine my proceedings; pray, be pleas'd

To shew in generous termes your griefes, since that

Your question's with your equall, who professes

To cleare his owne way with the minde and Sword

Of a true Gentleman.

PALAMON.

That thou durst, Arcite!

ARCITE.

My Coz, my Coz, you have beene well advertis'd

How much I dare, y'ave seene me use my Sword

Against th'advice of feare: sure, of another

You would not heare me doubted, but your silence

Should breake out, though i'th Sanctuary.

PALAMON.

Sir,

I have seene you move in such a place, which well

Might justifie your manhood; you were calld

A good knight and a bold; But the whole weeke's not faire,

If any day it rayne: Their valiant temper

Men loose when they encline to trecherie,

And then they fight like coupelld Beares, would fly

Were they not tyde.

ARCITE.

Kinsman, you might as well

Speake this and act it in your Glasse, as to

His eare which now disdaines you.

PALAMON.

Come up to me,

Quit me of these cold Gyves, give me a Sword,

Though it be rustie, and the charity

Of one meale lend me; Come before me then,

A good Sword in thy hand, and doe but say

That Emily is thine: I will forgive

The trespasse thou hast done me, yea, my life,

If then thou carry't, and brave soules in shades

That have dyde manly, which will seeke of me

Some newes from earth, they shall get none but this,

That thou art brave and noble.

ARCITE.

Be content:

Againe betake you to your hawthorne house;

With counsaile of the night, I will be here

With wholesome viands; these impediments

Will I file off; you shall have garments and

Perfumes to kill the smell o'th prison; after,

When you shall stretch your selfe and say but, 'Arcite,

I am in plight,' there shall be at your choyce

Both Sword and Armour.

PALAMON.

Oh you heavens, dares any

So noble beare a guilty busines! none

But onely Arcite, therefore none but Arcite

In this kinde is so bold.

ARCITE.

Sweete Palamon.

PALAMON.

I doe embrace you and your offer,—for

Your offer doo't I onely, Sir; your person,

Without hipocrisy I may not wish [Winde hornes of Cornets.]

More then my Swords edge ont.

ARCITE.

You heare the Hornes;

Enter your Musite least this match between's

Be crost, er met: give me your hand; farewell.

Ile bring you every needfull thing: I pray you,

Take comfort and be strong.

PALAMON.

Pray hold your promise;

And doe the deede with a bent brow: most certaine

You love me not, be rough with me, and powre

This oile out of your language; by this ayre,

I could for each word give a Cuffe, my stomach

Not reconcild by reason.

ARCITE.

Plainely spoken,

Yet pardon me hard language: when I spur [Winde hornes.]

My horse, I chide him not; content and anger

In me have but one face. Harke, Sir, they call

The scatterd to the Banket; you must guesse

I have an office there.

PALAMON.

Sir, your attendance

Cannot please heaven, and I know your office

Vnjustly is atcheev'd.

ARCITE.

If a good title,

I am perswaded this question sicke between's

By bleeding must be cur'd. I am a Suitour,

That to your Sword you will bequeath this plea

And talke of it no more.

PALAMON.

But this one word:

You are going now to gaze upon my Mistris,

For note you, mine she is—

ARCITE.

Nay, then.

PALAMON.

Nay, pray you,

You talke of feeding me to breed me strength:

You are going now to looke upon a Sun

That strengthens what it lookes on; there

You have a vantage ore me, but enjoy't till

I may enforce my remedy. Farewell.

[Exeunt.]

SCENE 2. (Another Part of the forest.)

[Enter Iaylors daughter alone.]

DAUGHTER.

He has mistooke the Brake I meant, is gone

After his fancy. Tis now welnigh morning;

No matter, would it were perpetuall night,

And darkenes Lord o'th world. Harke, tis a woolfe:

In me hath greife slaine feare, and but for one thing

I care for nothing, and that's Palamon.

I wreake not if the wolves would jaw me, so

He had this File: what if I hallowd for him?

I cannot hallow: if I whoop'd, what then?

If he not answeard, I should call a wolfe,

And doe him but that service. I have heard

Strange howles this live-long night, why may't not be

They have made prey of him? he has no weapons,

He cannot run, the Iengling of his Gives

Might call fell things to listen, who have in them

A sence to know a man unarmd, and can

Smell where resistance is. Ile set it downe

He's torne to peeces; they howld many together

And then they fed on him: So much for that,

Be bold to ring the Bell; how stand I then?

All's char'd when he is gone. No, no, I lye,

My Father's to be hang'd for his escape;

My selfe to beg, if I prizd life so much

As to deny my act, but that I would not,

Should I try death by dussons.—I am mop't,

Food tooke I none these two daies,

Sipt some water. I have not closd mine eyes

Save when my lids scowrd off their brine; alas,

Dissolue my life, Let not my sence unsettle,

Least I should drowne, or stab or hang my selfe.

O state of Nature, faile together in me,

Since thy best props are warpt! So, which way now?

The best way is the next way to a grave:

Each errant step beside is torment. Loe,

The Moone is down, the Cryckets chirpe, the Schreichowle

Calls in the dawne; all offices are done

Save what I faile in: But the point is this,

An end, and that is all.

[Exit.]

SCENE 3. (Same as Scene I.)

[Enter Arcite, with Meate, Wine, and Files.]

ARCITE.

I should be neere the place: hoa, Cosen Palamon.

[Enter Palamon.]

PALAMON.

Arcite?

ARCITE.

The same: I have brought you foode and files.

Come forth and feare not, here's no Theseus.

PALAMON.

Nor none so honest, Arcite.

ARCITE.

That's no matter,

Wee'l argue that hereafter: Come, take courage;

You shall not dye thus beastly: here, Sir, drinke;

I know you are faint: then ile talke further with you.

PALAMON.

Arcite, thou mightst now poyson me.

ARCITE.

I might,

But I must feare you first: Sit downe, and, good, now

No more of these vaine parlies; let us not,

Having our ancient reputation with us,

Make talke for Fooles and Cowards. To your health, &c.

PALAMON.

Doe.

ARCITE.

Pray, sit downe then; and let me entreate you,

By all the honesty and honour in you,

No mention of this woman: t'will disturbe us;

We shall have time enough.

PALAMON.

Well, Sir, Ile pledge you.

ARCITE.

Drinke a good hearty draught; it breeds good blood, man.

Doe not you feele it thaw you?

PALAMON.

Stay, Ile tell you after a draught or two more.

ARCITE.

Spare it not, the Duke has more, Cuz: Eate now.

PALAMON.

Yes.

ARCITE.

I am glad you have so good a stomach.

PALAMON.

I am gladder I have so good meate too't.

ARCITE.

Is't not mad lodging here in the wild woods, Cosen?

PALAMON.

Yes, for them that have wilde Consciences.

ARCITE.

How tasts your vittails? your hunger needs no sawce, I see.

PALAMON.

Not much;

But if it did, yours is too tart, sweete Cosen: what is this?

ARCITE.

Venison.

PALAMON.

Tis a lusty meate:

Giue me more wine; here, Arcite, to the wenches

We have known in our daies. The Lord Stewards daughter,

Doe you remember her?

ARCITE.

After you, Cuz.

PALAMON.

She lov'd a black-haird man.

ARCITE.

She did so; well, Sir.

PALAMON.

And I have heard some call him Arcite, and—

ARCITE.

Out with't, faith.

PALAMON.

She met him in an Arbour:

What did she there, Cuz? play o'th virginals?

ARCITE.

Something she did, Sir.

PALAMON.

Made her groane a moneth for't, or 2. or 3. or 10.

ARCITE.

The Marshals Sister

Had her share too, as I remember, Cosen,

Else there be tales abroade; you'l pledge her?

PALAMON.

Yes.

ARCITE.

A pretty broune wench t'is. There was a time

When yong men went a hunting, and a wood,

And a broade Beech: and thereby hangs a tale:—heigh ho!

PALAMON.

For Emily, upon my life! Foole,

Away with this straind mirth; I say againe,

That sigh was breathd for Emily; base Cosen,

Dar'st thou breake first?

ARCITE.

You are wide.

PALAMON.

By heaven and earth, ther's nothing in thee honest.

ARCITE.

Then Ile leave you: you are a Beast now.

PALAMON.

As thou makst me, Traytour.

ARCITE.

Ther's all things needfull, files and shirts, and perfumes:

Ile come againe some two howres hence, and bring

That that shall quiet all,

PALAMON.

A Sword and Armour?

ARCITE.

Feare me not; you are now too fowle; farewell.

Get off your Trinkets; you shall want nought.

PALAMON.

Sir, ha—

ARCITE.

Ile heare no more.

[Exit.]

PALAMON.

If he keepe touch, he dies for't.

[Exit.]

SCENE 4. (Another part of the forest.)

[Enter Iaylors daughter.]

DAUGHTER.

I am very cold, and all the Stars are out too,

The little Stars, and all, that looke like aglets:

The Sun has seene my Folly. Palamon!

Alas no; hees in heaven. Where am I now?

Yonder's the sea, and ther's a Ship; how't tumbles!

And ther's a Rocke lies watching under water;

Now, now, it beates upon it; now, now, now,

Ther's a leak sprung, a sound one, how they cry!

Spoon her before the winde, you'l loose all els:

Vp with a course or two, and take about, Boyes.

Good night, good night, y'ar gone.—I am very hungry.

Would I could finde a fine Frog; he would tell me

Newes from all parts o'th world, then would I make

A Carecke of a Cockle shell, and sayle

By east and North East to the King of Pigmes,

For he tels fortunes rarely. Now my Father,

Twenty to one, is trust up in a trice

To morrow morning; Ile say never a word.

[Sing.]

For ile cut my greene coat a foote above my knee, And ile clip my yellow lockes an inch below mine eie. hey, nonny, nonny, nonny, He's buy me a white Cut, forth for to ride And ile goe seeke him, throw the world that is so wide hey nonny, nonny, nonny.

O for a pricke now like a Nightingale,

To put my breast against. I shall sleepe like a Top else.

[Exit.]

SCENE 5. (Another part of the forest.)

[Enter a Schoole master, 4. Countrymen, and Bavian. 2. or 3. wenches, with a Taborer.]

SCHOOLMASTER.

Fy, fy, what tediosity, & disensanity is here among ye? have my Rudiments bin labourd so long with ye? milkd unto ye, and by a figure even the very plumbroth & marrow of my understanding laid upon ye? and do you still cry: where, and how, & wherfore? you most course freeze capacities, ye jane Iudgements, have I saide: thus let be, and there let be, and then let be, and no man understand mee? Proh deum, medius fidius, ye are all dunces! For why, here stand I, Here the Duke comes, there are you close in the Thicket; the Duke appeares, I meete him and unto him I utter learned things and many figures; he heares, and nods, and hums, and then cries: rare, and I goe forward; at length I fling my Cap up; marke there; then do you, as once did Meleager and the Bore, break comly out before him: like true lovers, cast your selves in a Body decently, and sweetly, by a figure trace and turne, Boyes.

1. COUNTREYMAN.

And sweetly we will doe it Master Gerrold.

2. COUNTREYMAN.

Draw up the Company. Where's the Taborour?

3. COUNTREYMAN.

Why, Timothy!

TABORER.

Here, my mad boyes, have at ye.

SCHOOLMASTER.

But I say, where's their women?

4. COUNTREYMAN.

Here's Friz and Maudline.

2. COUNTREYMAN.

And little Luce with the white legs, and bouncing Barbery.

1. COUNTREYMAN.

And freckeled Nel, that never faild her Master.

SCHOOLMASTER.

Wher be your Ribands, maids? swym with your Bodies

And carry it sweetly, and deliverly

And now and then a fauour, and a friske.

NEL.

Let us alone, Sir.

SCHOOLMASTER.

Wher's the rest o'th Musicke?

3. COUNTREYMAN.

Dispersd as you commanded.

SCHOOLMASTER.

Couple, then,

And see what's wanting; wher's the Bavian?

My friend, carry your taile without offence

Or scandall to the Ladies; and be sure

You tumble with audacity and manhood;

And when you barke, doe it with judgement.

BAVIAN.

Yes, Sir.

SCHOOLMASTER.

Quo usque tandem? Here is a woman wanting.

4. COUNTREYMAN.

We may goe whistle: all the fat's i'th fire.

SCHOOLMASTER.

We have,

As learned Authours utter, washd a Tile,

We have beene FATUUS, and laboured vainely.

2. COUNTREYMAN.

This is that scornefull peece, that scurvy hilding,

That gave her promise faithfully, she would be here,

Cicely the Sempsters daughter:

The next gloves that I give her shall be dog skin;

Nay and she faile me once—you can tell, Arcas,

She swore by wine and bread, she would not breake.

SCHOOLMASTER.

An Eele and woman,

A learned Poet sayes, unles by'th taile

And with thy teeth thou hold, will either faile.

In manners this was false position

1. COUNTREYMAN.

A fire ill take her; do's she flinch now?

3. COUNTREYMAN.

What

Shall we determine, Sir?

SCHOOLMASTER.

Nothing.

Our busines is become a nullity;

Yea, and a woefull, and a pittious nullity.

4. COUNTREYMAN.

Now when the credite of our Towne lay on it,

Now to be frampall, now to pisse o'th nettle!

Goe thy waies; ile remember thee, ile fit thee.

[Enter Iaylors daughter.]

DAUGHTER.

[Sings.]

The George alow came from the South,

From the coast of Barbary a.

And there he met with brave gallants of war

By one, by two, by three, a.

Well haild, well haild, you jolly gallants,

And whither now are you bound a?

O let me have your company

[Chaire and stooles out.]

Till (I) come to the sound a.

There was three fooles, fell out about an howlet:

The one sed it was an owle,

The other he sed nay,

The third he sed it was a hawke,

And her bels wer cut away.

3. COUNTREYMAN.

Ther's a dainty mad woman M(aiste)r

Comes i'th Nick, as mad as a march hare:

If wee can get her daunce, wee are made againe:

I warrant her, shee'l doe the rarest gambols.

1. COUNTREYMAN.

A mad woman? we are made, Boyes.

SCHOOLMASTER.

And are you mad, good woman?

DAUGHTER.

I would be sorry else;

Give me your hand.

SCHOOLMASTER.

Why?

DAUGHTER.

I can tell your fortune.

You are a foole: tell ten. I have pozd him: Buz!

Friend you must eate no whitebread; if you doe,

107

Your teeth will bleede extreamely. Shall we dance, ho?

I know you, y'ar a Tinker: Sirha Tinker,

Stop no more holes, but what you should.

SCHOOLMASTER.

Dij boni. A Tinker, Damzell?

DAUGHTER.

Or a Conjurer:

Raise me a devill now, and let him play

Quipassa o'th bels and bones.

SCHOOLMASTER.

Goe, take her,

And fluently perswade her to a peace:

Et opus exegi, quod nec Iouis ira, nec ignis.

Strike up, and leade her in.

2. COUNTREYMAN.

Come, Lasse, lets trip it.

DAUGHTER.

Ile leade. [Winde Hornes.]

3. COUNTREYMAN.

Doe, doe.

SCHOOLMASTER.

Perswasively, and cunningly: away, boyes,

[Ex. all but Schoolemaster.]

I heare the hornes: give me some meditation,

And marke your Cue.—Pallas inspire me.

[Enter Thes. Pir. Hip. Emil. Arcite, and traine.]

THESEUS.

This way the Stag tooke.

SCHOOLMASTER.

Stay, and edifie.

THESEUS.

What have we here?

PERITHOUS.

Some Countrey sport, upon my life, Sir.

THESEUS.

Well, Sir, goe forward, we will edifie.

Ladies, sit downe, wee'l stay it.

SCHOOLMASTER.

Thou, doughtie Duke, all haile: all haile, sweet Ladies.

THESEUS.

This is a cold beginning.

SCHOOLMASTER.

If you but favour, our Country pastime made is.

We are a few of those collected here,

That ruder Tongues distinguish villager;

And to say veritie, and not to fable,

We are a merry rout, or else a rable,

Or company, or, by a figure, Choris,

That fore thy dignitie will dance a Morris.

And I, that am the rectifier of all,

By title Pedagogus, that let fall

The Birch upon the breeches of the small ones,

And humble with a Ferula the tall ones,

Doe here present this Machine, or this frame:

And daintie Duke, whose doughtie dismall fame

From Dis to Dedalus, from post to pillar,

Is blowne abroad, helpe me thy poore well willer,

And with thy twinckling eyes looke right and straight

Vpon this mighty MORR—of mickle waight;

IS now comes in, which being glewd together,

Makes MORRIS, and the cause that we came hether.

The body of our sport, of no small study,

I first appeare, though rude, and raw, and muddy,

To speake before thy noble grace this tenner:

At whose great feete I offer up my penner.

The next the Lord of May and Lady bright,

The Chambermaid and Servingman by night

That seeke out silent hanging: Then mine Host

And his fat Spowse, that welcomes to their cost

The gauled Traveller, and with a beckning

Informes the Tapster to inflame the reckning:

Then the beast eating Clowne, and next the foole,

The Bavian, with long tayle and eke long toole,

Cum multis alijs that make a dance:

Say 'I,' and all shall presently advance.

THESEUS.

I, I, by any meanes, deere Domine.

PERITHOUS.

Produce.

(SCHOOLMASTER.)

Intrate, filij; Come forth, and foot it.—

[Musicke, Dance. Knocke for Schoole.]

[Enter the Dance.]

Ladies, if we have beene merry,

And have pleasd yee with a derry,

And a derry, and a downe,

Say the Schoolemaster's no Clowne:

Duke, if we have pleasd thee too,

And have done as good Boyes should doe,

Give us but a tree or twaine

For a Maypole, and againe,

Ere another yeare run out,

Wee'l make thee laugh and all this rout.

THESEUS.

Take 20., Domine; how does my sweet heart?

HIPPOLITA.

Never so pleasd, Sir.

EMILIA.

Twas an excellent dance, and for a preface

I never heard a better.

THESEUS.

Schoolemaster, I thanke you.—One see'em all rewarded.

PERITHOUS.

And heer's something to paint your Pole withall.

THESEUS.

Now to our sports againe.

SCHOOLMASTER.

May the Stag thou huntst stand long,

And thy dogs be swift and strong:

May they kill him without lets,

And the Ladies eate his dowsets!

Come, we are all made. [Winde Hornes.]

Dij Deoeq(ue) omnes, ye have danc'd rarely, wenches.

[Exeunt.]

SCENE 6. (Same as Scene III.)

[Enter Palamon from the Bush.]

PALAMON.

About this houre my Cosen gave his faith

To visit me againe, and with him bring

Two Swords, and two good Armors; if he faile,

He's neither man nor Souldier. When he left me,

I did not thinke a weeke could have restord

My lost strength to me, I was growne so low,

And Crest-falne with my wants: I thanke thee, Arcite,

Thou art yet a faire Foe; and I feele my selfe

With this refreshing, able once againe

To out dure danger: To delay it longer

Would make the world think, when it comes to hearing,

That I lay fatting like a Swine to fight,

And not a Souldier: Therefore, this blest morning

Shall be the last; and that Sword he refuses,

If it but hold, I kill him with; tis Iustice:

So love, and Fortune for me!—O, good morrow.

[Enter Arcite with Armors and Swords.]

ARCITE.

Good morrow, noble kinesman.

PALAMON.

I have put you to too much paines, Sir.

ARCITE.

That too much, faire Cosen,

Is but a debt to honour, and my duty.

PALAMON.

Would you were so in all, Sir; I could wish ye

As kinde a kinsman, as you force me finde

A beneficiall foe, that my embraces

Might thanke ye, not my blowes.

ARCITE.

I shall thinke either, well done,

A noble recompence.

PALAMON.

Then I shall quit you.

ARCITE.

Defy me in these faire termes, and you show

More then a Mistris to me, no more anger

As you love any thing that's honourable:

We were not bred to talke, man; when we are arm'd

And both upon our guards, then let our fury,

Like meeting of two tides, fly strongly from us,

And then to whom the birthright of this Beauty

114

Truely pertaines (without obbraidings, scornes,

Dispisings of our persons, and such powtings,

Fitter for Girles and Schooleboyes) will be seene

And quickly, yours, or mine: wilt please you arme, Sir,

Or if you feele your selfe not fitting yet

And furnishd with your old strength, ile stay, Cosen,

And ev'ry day discourse you into health,

As I am spard: your person I am friends with,

And I could wish I had not saide I lov'd her,

Though I had dide; But loving such a Lady

And justifying my Love, I must not fly from't.

PALAMON.

Arcite, thou art so brave an enemy,

That no man but thy Cosen's fit to kill thee:

I am well and lusty, choose your Armes.

ARCITE.

Choose you, Sir.

PALAMON.

Wilt thou exceede in all, or do'st thou doe it

To make me spare thee?

ARCITE.

If you thinke so, Cosen,

You are deceived, for as I am a Soldier,

I will not spare you.

PALAMON.

That's well said.

ARCITE.

You'l finde it.

PALAMON.

Then, as I am an honest man and love

With all the justice of affection,

Ile pay thee soundly. This ile take.

ARCITE.

That's mine, then;

Ile arme you first.

PALAMON.

Do: pray thee, tell me, Cosen,

Where gotst thou this good Armour?

ARCITE.

Tis the Dukes,

And to say true, I stole it; doe I pinch you?

PALAMON.

Noe.

ARCITE.

Is't not too heavie?

PALAMON.

I have worne a lighter,

But I shall make it serve.

ARCITE.

Ile buckl't close.

PALAMON.

By any meanes.

ARCITE.

You care not for a Grand guard?

PALAMON.

No, no; wee'l use no horses: I perceave

You would faine be at that Fight.

ARCITE.

I am indifferent.

PALAMON.

Faith, so am I: good Cosen, thrust the buckle

Through far enough.

ARCITE.

I warrant you.

PALAMON.

My Caske now.

ARCITE.

Will you fight bare-armd?

PALAMON.

We shall be the nimbler.

ARCITE.

But use your Gauntlets though; those are o'th least,

Prethee take mine, good Cosen.

PALAMON.

Thanke you, Arcite.

How doe I looke? am I falne much away?

ARCITE.

Faith, very little; love has usd you kindly.

PALAMON.

Ile warrant thee, Ile strike home.

ARCITE.

Doe, and spare not;

Ile give you cause, sweet Cosen.

PALAMON.

Now to you, Sir:

Me thinkes this Armor's very like that, Arcite,

Thou wor'st the day the 3. Kings fell, but lighter.

ARCITE.

That was a very good one; and that day,

I well remember, you outdid me, Cosen.

I never saw such valour: when you chargd

Vpon the left wing of the Enemie,

I spurd hard to come up, and under me

I had a right good horse.

PALAMON.

You had indeede; a bright Bay, I remember.

ARCITE.

Yes, but all

Was vainely labour'd in me; you outwent me,

Nor could my wishes reach you; yet a little

I did by imitation.

PALAMON.

More by vertue;

You are modest, Cosen.

ARCITE.

When I saw you charge first,

Me thought I heard a dreadfull clap of Thunder

Breake from the Troope.

PALAMON.

But still before that flew

The lightning of your valour. Stay a little,

Is not this peece too streight?

ARCITE.

No, no, tis well.

PALAMON.

I would have nothing hurt thee but my Sword,

A bruise would be dishonour.

ARCITE.

Now I am perfect.

PALAMON.

Stand off, then.

ARCITE.

Take my Sword, I hold it better.

PALAMON.

I thanke ye: No, keepe it; your life lyes on it.

Here's one; if it but hold, I aske no more

For all my hopes: My Cause and honour guard me!

[They bow severall wayes: then advance and stand.]

ARCITE.

And me my love! Is there ought else to say?

PALAMON.

This onely, and no more: Thou art mine Aunts Son,

And that blood we desire to shed is mutuall;

In me, thine, and in thee, mine. My Sword

Is in my hand, and if thou killst me,

The gods and I forgive thee; If there be

A place prepar'd for those that sleepe in honour,

I wish his wearie soule that falls may win it:

Fight bravely, Cosen; give me thy noble hand.

ARCITE.

Here, Palamon: This hand shall never more

Come neare thee with such friendship.

PALAMON.

I commend thee.

ARCITE.

If I fall, curse me, and say I was a coward,

For none but such dare die in these just Tryalls.

Once more farewell, my Cosen.

PALAMON.

Farewell, Arcite. [Fight.]

[Hornes within: they stand.]

ARCITE.

Loe, Cosen, loe, our Folly has undon us.

PALAMON.

Why?

ARCITE.

This is the Duke, a hunting as I told you.

If we be found, we are wretched. O retire

For honours sake, and safety presently

Into your Bush agen; Sir, we shall finde

Too many howres to dye in: gentle Cosen,

If you be seene you perish instantly

For breaking prison, and I, if you reveale me,

For my contempt. Then all the world will scorne us,

And say we had a noble difference,

But base disposers of it.

PALAMON.

No, no, Cosen,

I will no more be hidden, nor put off

This great adventure to a second Tryall:

I know your cunning, and I know your cause;

He that faints now, shame take him: put thy selfe

Vpon thy present guard—

ARCITE.

You are not mad?

PALAMON.

Or I will make th'advantage of this howre

Mine owne, and what to come shall threaten me,

I feare lesse then my fortune: know, weake Cosen,

I love Emilia, and in that ile bury

Thee, and all crosses else.

ARCITE.

Then, come what can come,

Thou shalt know, Palamon, I dare as well

Die, as discourse, or sleepe: Onely this feares me,

The law will have the honour of our ends.

Have at thy life.

PALAMON.

Looke to thine owne well, Arcite. [Fight againe. Hornes.]

   [Enter Theseus, Hipolita, Emilia, Perithous and traine.]

THESEUS.

What ignorant and mad malicious Traitors,

Are you, That gainst the tenor of my Lawes

Are making Battaile, thus like Knights appointed,

Without my leave, and Officers of Armes?

By Castor, both shall dye.

PALAMON.

Hold thy word, Theseus.

We are certainly both Traitors, both despisers

Of thee and of thy goodnesse: I am Palamon,

That cannot love thee, he that broke thy Prison;

Thinke well what that deserves: and this is Arcite,

A bolder Traytor never trod thy ground,

A Falser neu'r seem'd friend: This is the man

Was begd and banish'd; this is he contemnes thee

And what thou dar'st doe, and in this disguise

Against thy owne Edict followes thy Sister,

That fortunate bright Star, the faire Emilia,

Whose servant, (if there be a right in seeing,

And first bequeathing of the soule to) justly

I am, and, which is more, dares thinke her his.

This treacherie, like a most trusty Lover,

I call'd him now to answer; if thou bee'st,

As thou art spoken, great and vertuous,

The true descider of all injuries,

Say, 'Fight againe,' and thou shalt see me, Theseus,

Doe such a Iustice, thou thy selfe wilt envie.

Then take my life; Ile wooe thee too't.

PERITHOUS.

O heaven,

What more then man is this!

THESEUS.

I have sworne.

ARCITE.

We seeke not

Thy breath of mercy, Theseus. Tis to me

A thing as soone to dye, as thee to say it,

And no more mov'd: where this man calls me Traitor,

Let me say thus much: if in love be Treason,

In service of so excellent a Beutie,

As I love most, and in that faith will perish,

As I have brought my life here to confirme it,

As I have serv'd her truest, worthiest,

As I dare kill this Cosen, that denies it,

So let me be most Traitor, and ye please me.

For scorning thy Edict, Duke, aske that Lady

Why she is faire, and why her eyes command me

Stay here to love her; and if she say 'Traytor,'

I am a villaine fit to lye unburied.

PALAMON.

Thou shalt have pitty of us both, o Theseus,

If unto neither thou shew mercy; stop

(As thou art just) thy noble eare against us.

As thou art valiant, for thy Cosens soule

Whose 12. strong labours crowne his memory,

Lets die together, at one instant, Duke,

Onely a little let him fall before me,

That I may tell my Soule he shall not have her.

THESEUS.

I grant your wish, for, to say true, your Cosen

Has ten times more offended; for I gave him

More mercy then you found, Sir, your offenses

Being no more then his. None here speake for 'em,

For, ere the Sun set, both shall sleepe for ever.

HIPPOLITA.

Alas the pitty! now or never, Sister,

Speake, not to be denide; That face of yours

Will beare the curses else of after ages

For these lost Cosens.

EMILIA.

In my face, deare Sister,

I finde no anger to 'em, nor no ruyn;

The misadventure of their owne eyes kill 'em;

Yet that I will be woman, and have pitty,

My knees shall grow to'th ground but Ile get mercie.

Helpe me, deare Sister; in a deede so vertuous

The powers of all women will be with us.

Most royall Brother—

HIPPOLITA.

Sir, by our tye of Marriage—

EMILIA.

By your owne spotlesse honour—

HIPPOLITA.

By that faith,

That faire hand, and that honest heart you gave me.

EMILIA.

By that you would have pitty in another,

By your owne vertues infinite.

HIPPOLITA.

By valour,

By all the chaste nights I have ever pleasd you.

THESEUS.

These are strange Conjurings.

PERITHOUS.

Nay, then, Ile in too:

By all our friendship, Sir, by all our dangers,

By all you love most: warres and this sweet Lady.

EMILIA.

By that you would have trembled to deny,

A blushing Maide.

HIPPOLITA.

By your owne eyes: By strength,

In which you swore I went beyond all women,

Almost all men, and yet I yeelded, Theseus.

PERITHOUS.

To crowne all this: By your most noble soule,

Which cannot want due mercie, I beg first.

HIPPOLITA.

Next, heare my prayers.

EMILIA.

Last, let me intreate, Sir.

PERITHOUS.

For mercy.

HIPPOLITA.

Mercy.

EMILIA.

Mercy on these Princes.

THESEUS.

Ye make my faith reele: Say I felt

Compassion to'em both, how would you place it?

EMILIA.

Vpon their lives: But with their banishments.

THESEUS.

You are a right woman, Sister; you have pitty,

But want the vnderstanding where to use it.

If you desire their lives, invent a way

Safer then banishment: Can these two live

And have the agony of love about 'em,

And not kill one another? Every day

They'ld fight about you; howrely bring your honour

In publique question with their Swords. Be wise, then,

And here forget 'em; it concernes your credit

And my oth equally: I have said they die;

Better they fall by'th law, then one another.

Bow not my honor.

EMILIA.

O my noble Brother,

That oth was rashly made, and in your anger,

Your reason will not hold it; if such vowes

Stand for expresse will, all the world must perish.

Beside, I have another oth gainst yours,

Of more authority, I am sure more love,

Not made in passion neither, but good heede.

THESEUS.

What is it, Sister?

PERITHOUS.

Vrge it home, brave Lady.

EMILIA.

That you would nev'r deny me any thing

Fit for my modest suit, and your free granting:

I tye you to your word now; if ye fall in't,

Thinke how you maime your honour,

(For now I am set a begging, Sir, I am deafe

To all but your compassion.) How, their lives

Might breed the ruine of my name, Opinion!

Shall any thing that loves me perish for me?

That were a cruell wisedome; doe men proyne

The straight yong Bowes that blush with thousand Blossoms,

Because they may be rotten? O Duke Theseus,

The goodly Mothers that have groand for these,

And all the longing Maides that ever lov'd,

If your vow stand, shall curse me and my Beauty,

And in their funerall songs for these two Cosens

Despise my crueltie, and cry woe worth me,

Till I am nothing but the scorne of women;

For heavens sake save their lives, and banish 'em.

THESEUS.

On what conditions?

EMILIA.

Sweare'em never more

To make me their Contention, or to know me,

To tread upon thy Dukedome; and to be,

Where ever they shall travel, ever strangers

To one another.

PALAMON.

Ile be cut a peeces

Before I take this oth: forget I love her?

O all ye gods dispise me, then! Thy Banishment

I not mislike, so we may fairely carry

Our Swords and cause along: else, never trifle,

But take our lives, Duke: I must love and will,

And for that love must and dare kill this Cosen

On any peece the earth has.

THESEUS.

Will you, Arcite,

Take these conditions?

PALAMON.

He's a villaine, then.

PERITHOUS.

These are men.

ARCITE.

No, never, Duke: Tis worse to me than begging

To take my life so basely; though I thinke

I never shall enjoy her, yet ile preserve

The honour of affection, and dye for her,

Make death a Devill.

THESEUS.

What may be done? for now I feele compassion.

PERITHOUS.

Let it not fall agen, Sir.

THESEUS.

Say, Emilia,

If one of them were dead, as one must, are you

Content to take th'other to your husband?

They cannot both enjoy you; They are Princes

As goodly as your owne eyes, and as noble

As ever fame yet spoke of; looke upon 'em,

And if you can love, end this difference.

I give consent; are you content too, Princes?

BOTH.

With all our soules.

THESEUS.

He that she refuses

Must dye, then.

BOTH.

Any death thou canst invent, Duke.

PALAMON.

If I fall from that mouth, I fall with favour,

And Lovers yet unborne shall blesse my ashes.

ARCITE.

If she refuse me, yet my grave will wed me,

And Souldiers sing my Epitaph.

THESEUS.

Make choice, then.

EMILIA.

I cannot, Sir, they are both too excellent:

For me, a hayre shall never fall of these men.

HIPPOLITA.

What will become of 'em?

THESEUS.

Thus I ordaine it;

And by mine honor, once againe, it stands,

Or both shall dye:—You shall both to your Countrey,

And each within this moneth, accompanied

With three faire Knights, appeare againe in this place,

In which Ile plant a Pyramid; and whether,

Before us that are here, can force his Cosen

By fayre and knightly strength to touch the Pillar,

He shall enjoy her: the other loose his head,

And all his friends; Nor shall he grudge to fall,

Nor thinke he dies with interest in this Lady:

Will this content yee?

PALAMON.

Yes: here, Cosen Arcite,

I am friends againe, till that howre.

ARCITE.

I embrace ye.

THESEUS.

Are you content, Sister?

EMILIA.

Yes, I must, Sir,

Els both miscarry.

THESEUS.

Come, shake hands againe, then;

And take heede, as you are Gentlemen, this Quarrell

Sleepe till the howre prefixt; and hold your course.

PALAMON.

We dare not faile thee, Theseus.

THESEUS.

Come, Ile give ye

Now usage like to Princes, and to Friends:

When ye returne, who wins, Ile settle heere;

Who looses, yet Ile weepe upon his Beere.

[Exeunt.]

ACT IV

SCENE 1. (Athens. A room in the prison.)

[Enter Iailor and his friend.]

IAILOR.

Heare you no more? was nothing saide of me

Concerning the escape of Palamon?

Good Sir, remember.

1. FRIEND.

Nothing that I heard,

For I came home before the busines

Was fully ended: Yet I might perceive,

Ere I departed, a great likelihood

Of both their pardons: For Hipolita,

And faire-eyd Emilie, upon their knees

Begd with such hansom pitty, that the Duke

Me thought stood staggering, whether he should follow

His rash oth, or the sweet compassion

Of those two Ladies; and to second them,

That truely noble Prince Perithous,

Halfe his owne heart, set in too, that I hope

All shall be well: Neither heard I one question

Of your name or his scape.

[Enter 2. Friend.]

IAILOR.

Pray heaven it hold so.

2. FRIEND.

Be of good comfort, man; I bring you newes,

Good newes.

IAILOR.

They are welcome,

2. FRIEND.

Palamon has cleerd you,

And got your pardon, and discoverd how

And by whose meanes he escapt, which was your Daughters,

Whose pardon is procurd too; and the Prisoner,

Not to be held ungratefull to her goodnes,

Has given a summe of money to her Marriage,

A large one, ile assure you.

IAILOR.

Ye are a good man

And ever bring good newes.

1. FRIEND.

How was it ended?

2. FRIEND.

Why, as it should be; they that nev'r begd

But they prevaild, had their suites fairely granted,

The prisoners have their lives.

1. FRIEND.

I knew t'would be so.

2. FRIEND.

But there be new conditions, which you'l heare of

At better time.

IAILOR.

I hope they are good.

2. FRIEND.

They are honourable,

How good they'l prove, I know not.

[Enter Wooer.]

1. FRIEND.

T'will be knowne.

WOOER.

Alas, Sir, wher's your Daughter?

IAILOR.

Why doe you aske?

WOOER.

O, Sir, when did you see her?

2. FRIEND.

How he lookes?

IAILOR.

This morning.

WOOER.

Was she well? was she in health, Sir?

When did she sleepe?

1. FRIEND.

These are strange Questions.

IAILOR.

I doe not thinke she was very well, for now

You make me minde her, but this very day

I ask'd her questions, and she answered me

So farre from what she was, so childishly,

So sillily, as if she were a foole,

An Inocent, and I was very angry.

But what of her, Sir?

WOOER.

Nothing but my pitty;

But you must know it, and as good by me

As by an other that lesse loves her—

IAILOR.

Well, Sir.

1. FRIEND.

Not right?

2. FRIEND.

Not well?

WOOER.

No, Sir, not well.

Tis too true, she is mad.

1. FRIEND.

It cannot be.

WOOER.

Beleeve, you'l finde it so.

IAILOR.

I halfe suspected

What you (have) told me: the gods comfort her:

Either this was her love to Palamon,

Or feare of my miscarrying on his scape,

Or both.

WOOER.

Tis likely.

IAILOR.

But why all this haste, Sir?

WOOER.

Ile tell you quickly. As I late was angling

In the great Lake that lies behind the Pallace,

From the far shore, thicke set with reedes and Sedges,

As patiently I was attending sport,

I heard a voyce, a shrill one, and attentive

I gave my eare, when I might well perceive

T'was one that sung, and by the smallnesse of it

A boy or woman. I then left my angle

To his owne skill, came neere, but yet perceivd not

Who made the sound, the rushes and the Reeds

Had so encompast it: I laide me downe

And listned to the words she sung, for then,

Through a small glade cut by the Fisher men,

I saw it was your Daughter.

IAILOR.

Pray, goe on, Sir?

WOOER.

She sung much, but no sence; onely I heard her

Repeat this often: 'Palamon is gone,

Is gone to'th wood to gather Mulberies;

Ile finde him out to morrow.'

1. FRIEND.

Pretty soule.

WOOER.

'His shackles will betray him, hee'l be taken,

And what shall I doe then? Ile bring a beavy,

A hundred blacke eyd Maides, that love as I doe,

With Chaplets on their heads of Daffadillies,

With cherry-lips, and cheekes of Damaske Roses,

And all wee'l daunce an Antique fore the Duke,

And beg his pardon.' Then she talk'd of you, Sir;

That you must loose your head to morrow morning,

And she must gather flowers to bury you,

And see the house made handsome: then she sung

Nothing but 'Willow, willow, willow,' and betweene

Ever was, 'Palamon, faire Palamon,'

And 'Palamon was a tall yong man.' The place

Was knee deepe where she sat; her careles Tresses

A wreathe of bull-rush rounded; about her stucke

Thousand fresh water flowers of severall cullors,

That me thought she appeard like the faire Nimph

That feedes the lake with waters, or as Iris

Newly dropt downe from heaven; Rings she made

Of rushes that grew by, and to 'em spoke

The prettiest posies: 'Thus our true love's tide,'

'This you may loose, not me,' and many a one:

And then she wept, and sung againe, and sigh'd,

And with the same breath smil'd, and kist her hand.

2. FRIEND.

Alas, what pitty it is!

WOOER.

I made in to her.

She saw me, and straight sought the flood; I sav'd her,

And set her safe to land: when presently

She slipt away, and to the Citty made,

With such a cry and swiftnes, that, beleeve me,

Shee left me farre behinde her; three or foure

I saw from farre off crosse her, one of 'em

I knew to be your brother; where she staid,

And fell, scarce to be got away: I left them with her,

[Enter Brother, Daughter, and others.]

And hether came to tell you. Here they are.

DAUGHTER. [sings.]

May you never more enjoy the light, &c.

Is not this a fine Song?

BROTHER.

O, a very fine one.

DAUGHTER.

I can sing twenty more.

BROTHER.

I thinke you can.

DAUGHTER.

Yes, truely, can I; I can sing the Broome,

And Bony Robin. Are not you a tailour?

BROTHER.

Yes.

DAUGHTER.

Wher's my wedding Gowne?

BROTHER.

Ile bring it to morrow.

DAUGHTER.

Doe, very rarely; I must be abroad else

To call the Maides, and pay the Minstrels,

For I must loose my Maydenhead by cock-light;

Twill never thrive else.

[Singes.] O faire, oh sweete, &c.

BROTHER.

You must ev'n take it patiently.

IAILOR.

Tis true.

DAUGHTER.

Good ev'n, good men; pray, did you ever heare

Of one yong Palamon?

IAILOR.

Yes, wench, we know him.

DAUGHTER.

Is't not a fine yong Gentleman?

IAILOR.

Tis Love.

BROTHER.

By no meane crosse her; she is then distemperd

Far worse then now she showes.

1. FRIEND.

Yes, he's a fine man.

DAUGHTER.

O, is he so? you have a Sister?

1. FRIEND.

Yes.

DAUGHTER.

But she shall never have him, tell her so,

For a tricke that I know; y'had best looke to her,

For if she see him once, she's gone, she's done,

And undon in an howre. All the young Maydes

Of our Towne are in love with him, but I laugh at 'em

And let 'em all alone; Is't not a wise course?

1. FRIEND.

Yes.

DAUGHTER.

There is at least two hundred now with child by him—

There must be fowre; yet I keepe close for all this,

Close as a Cockle; and all these must be Boyes,

He has the tricke on't, and at ten yeares old

They must be all gelt for Musitians,

And sing the wars of Theseus.

2. FRIEND.

This is strange.

DAUGHTER.

As ever you heard, but say nothing.

1. FRIEND.

No.

DAUGHTER.

They come from all parts of the Dukedome to him;

Ile warrant ye, he had not so few last night

As twenty to dispatch: hee'l tickl't up

In two howres, if his hand be in.

IAILOR.

She's lost

Past all cure.

BROTHER.

Heaven forbid, man.

DAUGHTER.

Come hither, you are a wise man.

1. FRIEND.

Do's she know him?

2. FRIEND.

No, would she did.

DAUGHTER.

You are master of a Ship?

IAILOR.

Yes.

DAUGHTER.

Wher's your Compasse?

IAILOR.

Heere.

DAUGHTER.

Set it too'th North.

And now direct your course to'th wood, wher Palamon

Lyes longing for me; For the Tackling

Let me alone; Come, waygh, my hearts, cheerely!

ALL.

Owgh, owgh, owgh, tis up, the wind's faire,

Top the Bowling, out with the maine saile;

Wher's your Whistle, Master?

BROTHER.

Lets get her in.

IAILOR.

Vp to the top, Boy.

BROTHER.

Wher's the Pilot?

1. FRIEND.

Heere.

DAUGHTER.

What ken'st thou?

2. FRIEND.

A faire wood.

DAUGHTER.

Beare for it, master: take about! [Singes.]

When Cinthia with her borrowed light, &c.

[Exeunt.]

SCENE 2. (A Room in the Palace.)

[Enter Emilia alone, with 2. Pictures.]

EMILIA.

Yet I may binde those wounds up, that must open

And bleed to death for my sake else; Ile choose,

And end their strife: Two such yong hansom men

Shall never fall for me, their weeping Mothers,

Following the dead cold ashes of their Sonnes,

Shall never curse my cruelty. Good heaven,

What a sweet face has Arcite! if wise nature,

With all her best endowments, all those beuties

She sowes into the birthes of noble bodies,

Were here a mortall woman, and had in her

The coy denialls of yong Maydes, yet doubtles,

She would run mad for this man: what an eye,

Of what a fyry sparkle, and quick sweetnes,

Has this yong Prince! Here Love himselfe sits smyling,

Iust such another wanton Ganimead

Set Jove a fire with, and enforcd the god

Snatch up the goodly Boy, and set him by him

A shining constellation: What a brow,

Of what a spacious Majesty, he carries!

Arch'd like the great eyd Iuno's, but far sweeter,

Smoother then Pelops Shoulder! Fame and honour,

Me thinks, from hence, as from a Promontory

Pointed in heaven, should clap their wings, and sing

To all the under world the Loves and Fights

Of gods, and such men neere 'em. Palamon

Is but his foyle, to him a meere dull shadow:

Hee's swarth and meagre, of an eye as heavy

As if he had lost his mother; a still temper,

No stirring in him, no alacrity,

Of all this sprightly sharpenes not a smile;

Yet these that we count errours may become him:

Narcissus was a sad Boy, but a heavenly:—

Oh who can finde the bent of womans fancy?

I am a Foole, my reason is lost in me;

I have no choice, and I have ly'd so lewdly

That women ought to beate me. On my knees

I aske thy pardon, Palamon; thou art alone,

And only beutifull, and these the eyes,

These the bright lamps of beauty, that command

And threaten Love, and what yong Mayd dare crosse 'em?

What a bold gravity, and yet inviting,

Has this browne manly face! O Love, this only

149

From this howre is Complexion: Lye there, Arcite,

Thou art a changling to him, a meere Gipsey,

And this the noble Bodie. I am sotted,

Vtterly lost: My Virgins faith has fled me;

For if my brother but even now had ask'd me

Whether I lov'd, I had run mad for Arcite;

Now, if my Sister, More for Palamon.

Stand both together: Now, come aske me, Brother.—

Alas, I know not! Aske me now, sweet Sister;—

I may goe looke. What a meere child is Fancie,

That, having two faire gawdes of equall sweetnesse,

Cannot distinguish, but must crie for both.

[Enter (a) Gent(leman.)]

EMILIA.

How now, Sir?

GENTLEMAN.

From the Noble Duke your Brother,

Madam, I bring you newes: The Knights are come.

EMILIA.

To end the quarrell?

GENTLEMAN.

Yes.

EMILIA.

Would I might end first:

What sinnes have I committed, chast Diana,

That my unspotted youth must now be soyld

With blood of Princes? and my Chastitie

Be made the Altar, where the lives of Lovers

(Two greater and two better never yet

Made mothers joy) must be the sacrifice

To my unhappy Beautie?

    [Enter Theseus, Hipolita, Perithous and attendants.]

THESEUS.

Bring 'em in

Quickly, By any meanes; I long to see 'em.—

Your two contending Lovers are return'd,

And with them their faire Knights: Now, my faire Sister,

You must love one of them.

EMILIA.

I had rather both,

So neither for my sake should fall untimely.

    [Enter Messenger. (Curtis.)]

THESEUS.

Who saw 'em?

PERITHOUS.

I, a while.

GENTLEMAN.

151

And I.

THESEUS.

From whence come you, Sir?

MESSENGER.

From the Knights.

THESEUS.

Pray, speake,

You that have seene them, what they are.

MESSENGER.

I will, Sir,

And truly what I thinke: Six braver spirits

Then these they have brought, (if we judge by the outside)

I never saw, nor read of. He that stands

In the first place with Arcite, by his seeming,

Should be a stout man, by his face a Prince,

(His very lookes so say him) his complexion,

Nearer a browne, than blacke, sterne, and yet noble,

Which shewes him hardy, fearelesse, proud of dangers:

The circles of his eyes show fire within him,

And as a heated Lyon, so he lookes;

His haire hangs long behind him, blacke and shining

Like Ravens wings: his shoulders broad and strong,

Armd long and round, and on his Thigh a Sword

Hung by a curious Bauldricke, when he frownes

To seale his will with: better, o'my conscience

Was never Souldiers friend.

THESEUS.

Thou ha'st well describde him.

PERITHOUS.

Yet a great deale short,

Me thinkes, of him that's first with Palamon.

THESEUS.

Pray, speake him, friend.

PERITHOUS.

I ghesse he is a Prince too,

And, if it may be, greater; for his show

Has all the ornament of honour in't:

Hee's somewhat bigger, then the Knight he spoke of,

But of a face far sweeter; His complexion

Is (as a ripe grape) ruddy: he has felt,

Without doubt, what he fights for, and so apter

To make this cause his owne: In's face appeares

All the faire hopes of what he undertakes,

And when he's angry, then a setled valour

(Not tainted with extreames) runs through his body,

And guides his arme to brave things: Feare he cannot,

He shewes no such soft temper; his head's yellow,

Hard hayr'd, and curld, thicke twind like Ivy tods,

Not to undoe with thunder; In his face

The liverie of the warlike Maide appeares,

Pure red, and white, for yet no beard has blest him.

And in his rowling eyes sits victory,

As if she ever ment to court his valour:

His Nose stands high, a Character of honour.

His red lips, after fights, are fit for Ladies.

EMILIA.

Must these men die too?

PERITHOUS.

When he speakes, his tongue

Sounds like a Trumpet; All his lyneaments

Are as a man would wish 'em, strong and cleane,

He weares a well-steeld Axe, the staffe of gold;

His age some five and twenty.

MESSENGER.

Ther's another,

A little man, but of a tough soule, seeming

As great as any: fairer promises

In such a Body yet I never look'd on.

PERITHOUS.

O, he that's freckle fac'd?

MESSENGER.

The same, my Lord;

Are they not sweet ones?

PERITHOUS.

Yes, they are well.

MESSENGER.

Me thinkes,

Being so few, and well disposd, they show

Great, and fine art in nature: he's white hair'd,

Not wanton white, but such a manly colour

Next to an aborne; tough, and nimble set,

Which showes an active soule; his armes are brawny,

Linde with strong sinewes: To the shoulder peece

Gently they swell, like women new conceav'd,

Which speakes him prone to labour, never fainting

Vnder the waight of Armes; stout harted, still,

But when he stirs, a Tiger; he's gray eyd,

Which yeelds compassion where he conquers: sharpe

To spy advantages, and where he finds 'em,

He's swift to make 'em his: He do's no wrongs,

Nor takes none; he's round fac'd, and when he smiles

He showes a Lover, when he frownes, a Souldier:

About his head he weares the winners oke,

And in it stucke the favour of his Lady:

His age, some six and thirtie. In his hand

He beares a charging Staffe, embost with silver.

THESEUS.

Are they all thus?

PERITHOUS.

They are all the sonnes of honour.

THESEUS.

Now, as I have a soule, I long to see'em.

Lady, you shall see men fight now.

HIPPOLITA.

I wish it,

But not the cause, my Lord; They would show

Bravely about the Titles of two Kingdomes;

Tis pitty Love should be so tyrannous:

O my soft harted Sister, what thinke you?

Weepe not, till they weepe blood, Wench; it must be.

THESEUS.

You have steel'd 'em with your Beautie.—Honord Friend,

To you I give the Feild; pray, order it

Fitting the persons that must use it.

PERITHOUS.

Yes, Sir.

THESEUS.

Come, Ile goe visit 'em: I cannot stay,

Their fame has fir'd me so; Till they appeare.

Good Friend, be royall.

PERITHOUS.

There shall want no bravery.

EMILIA.

Poore wench, goe weepe, for whosoever wins,

Looses a noble Cosen for thy sins.

[Exeunt.]

SCENE 3. (A room in the prison.)

[Enter Iailor, Wooer, Doctor.]

DOCTOR.

Her distraction is more at some time of the Moone, then at other some, is it not?

IAILOR.

She is continually in a harmelesse distemper, sleepes little, altogether without appetite, save often drinking, dreaming of another world, and a better; and what broken peece of matter so'ere she's about, the name Palamon lardes it, that she farces ev'ry busines withall, fyts it to every question.—

[Enter Daughter.]

Looke where shee comes, you shall perceive her behaviour.

DAUGHTER.

I have forgot it quite; The burden on't, was DOWNE A, DOWNE A, and pend by no worse man, then Giraldo, Emilias Schoolemaster; he's as Fantasticall too, as ever he may goe upon's legs,—for in the next world will Dido see Palamon, and then will she be out of love with Eneas.

DOCTOR.

What stuffs here? pore soule!

IAILOR.

Ev'n thus all day long.

DAUGHTER.

Now for this Charme, that I told you of: you must bring a peece of silver on the tip of your tongue, or no ferry: then, if it be your chance to come where the blessed spirits, as ther's a sight now—we maids that have our Lyvers perish'd, crakt to peeces with Love, we shall come there, and doe nothing all day long but picke flowers with Proserpine; then will I make Palamon a Nosegay; then let him marke me,—then—

DOCTOR.

How prettily she's amisse? note her a little further.

DAUGHTER.

Faith, ile tell you, sometime we goe to Barly breake, we of the blessed; alas, tis a sore life they have i'th other place, such burning, frying, boyling, hissing, howling, chattring, cursing, oh they have shrowd measure! take heede; if one be mad, or hang or drowne themselves, thither they goe, Iupiter blesse vs, and there shall we be put in a Caldron of lead, and Vsurers grease, amongst a whole million of cutpurses, and there boyle like a Gamon of Bacon that will never be enough.

[Exit.]

DOCTOR.

How her braine coynes!

DAUGHTER.

Lords and Courtiers, that have got maids with Child, they are in this place: they shall stand in fire up to the Nav'le, and in yce up to'th hart, and there th'offending part burnes, and the deceaving part freezes; in troth, a very greevous punishment, as one would thinke, for such a Trifle; beleve me, one would marry a leaprous witch, to be rid on't, Ile assure you.

DOCTOR.

How she continues this fancie! Tis not an engraffed Madnesse, but a most thicke, and profound mellencholly.

DAUGHTER.

To heare there a proud Lady, and a proud Citty wiffe, howle together! I were a beast and il'd call it good sport: one cries, 'O this smoake!' another,

159

'this fire!' One cries, 'O, that ever I did it behind the arras!' and then howles; th'other curses a suing fellow and her garden house. [Sings] I will be true, my stars, my fate, &c.

[Exit Daugh.]

IAILOR.

What thinke you of her, Sir?

DOCTOR.

I thinke she has a perturbed minde, which I cannot minister to.

IAILOR.

Alas, what then?

DOCTOR.

Vnderstand you, she ever affected any man, ere she beheld

Palamon?

IAILOR.

I was once, Sir, in great hope she had fixd her liking on this gentleman, my friend.

WOOER.

I did thinke so too, and would account I had a great pen-worth on't, to give halfe my state, that both she and I at this present stood unfainedly on the same tearmes.

DOCTOR.

That intemprat surfeit of her eye hath distemperd the other sences: they may returne and settle againe to execute their preordaind faculties, but they are now in a most extravagant vagary. This you must doe: Confine her to a place, where the light may rather seeme to steale in, then be permitted; take vpon you (yong Sir, her friend) the name of Palamon; say you come to eate with her, and to commune of Love; this will catch her attention, for this her minde beates upon; other objects that are inserted tweene her minde and eye become the prankes and friskins of her madnes; Sing to her such greene songs of Love, as she sayes Palamon hath sung in prison; Come to her, stucke in as sweet flowers as the season is mistres of, and thereto make an addition of som other compounded odours, which are grateful to the sence: all this shall become Palamon, for Palamon can sing, and Palamon is sweet, and ev'ry good thing: desire to eate with her, carve her, drinke to her, and still among, intermingle your petition of grace and acceptance into her favour: Learne what Maides have beene her companions and play-pheeres, and let them repaire to her with Palamon in their mouthes, and appeare with tokens, as if they suggested for him. It is a falsehood she is in, which is with falsehood to be combated. This may bring her to eate, to sleepe, and reduce what's now out of square in her, into their former law, and regiment; I have seene it approved, how many times I know not, but to make the number more, I have great hope in this. I will, betweene the passages of this project, come in with my applyance: Let us put it in execution, and hasten the successe, which, doubt not, will bring forth comfort.

[Florish. Exeunt.]

ACT V

SCENE 1. (Before the Temples of Mars, Venus, and Diana.)

[Enter Thesius, Perithous, Hipolita, attendants.]

THESEUS.

Now let'em enter, and before the gods

Tender their holy prayers: Let the Temples

Burne bright with sacred fires, and the Altars

In hallowed clouds commend their swelling Incense

To those above us: Let no due be wanting; [Florish of Cornets.]

They have a noble worke in hand, will honour

The very powers that love 'em.

[Enter Palamon and Arcite, and their Knights.]

PERITHOUS.

Sir, they enter.

THESEUS.

You valiant and strong harted Enemies,

You royall German foes, that this day come

To blow that furnesse out that flames betweene ye:

Lay by your anger for an houre, and dove-like,

Before the holy Altars of your helpers,

(The all feard gods) bow downe your stubborne bodies.

Your ire is more than mortall; So your helpe be,

And as the gods regard ye, fight with Iustice;

Ile leave you to your prayers, and betwixt ye

I part my wishes.

PERITHOUS.

Honour crowne the worthiest.

[Exit Theseus, and his traine.]

PALAMON.

The glasse is running now that cannot finish

Till one of us expire: Thinke you but thus,

That were there ought in me which strove to show

Mine enemy in this businesse, wer't one eye

Against another, Arme opprest by Arme,

I would destroy th'offender, Coz, I would,

Though parcell of my selfe: Then from this gather

How I should tender you.

ARCITE.

I am in labour

To push your name, your auncient love, our kindred

Out of my memory; and i'th selfe same place

To seate something I would confound: So hoyst we

The sayles, that must these vessells port even where

The heavenly Lymiter pleases.

PALAMON.

You speake well;

Before I turne, Let me embrace thee, Cosen:

This I shall never doe agen.

ARCITE.

One farewell.

PALAMON.

Why, let it be so: Farewell, Coz.

[Exeunt Palamon and his Knights.]

ARCITE.

Farewell, Sir.—

Knights, Kinsemen, Lovers, yea, my Sacrifices,

True worshippers of Mars, whose spirit in you

Expells the seedes of feare, and th'apprehension

Which still is farther off it, Goe with me

Before the god of our profession: There

Require of him the hearts of Lyons, and

The breath of Tigers, yea, the fearcenesse too,

Yea, the speed also,—to goe on, I meane,

Else wish we to be Snayles: you know my prize

Must be drag'd out of blood; force and great feate

Must put my Garland on, where she stickes

The Queene of Flowers: our intercession then

Must be to him that makes the Campe a Cestron

Brymd with the blood of men: give me your aide

And bend your spirits towards him. [They kneele.]

Thou mighty one, that with thy power hast turnd

Greene Neptune into purple, (whose Approach)

Comets prewarne, whose havocke in vaste Feild

Vnearthed skulls proclaime, whose breath blowes downe,

The teeming Ceres foyzon, who doth plucke

With hand armypotent from forth blew clowdes

The masond Turrets, that both mak'st and break'st

The stony girthes of Citties: me thy puple,

Yongest follower of thy Drom, instruct this day

With military skill, that to thy lawde

I may advance my Streamer, and by thee,

Be stil'd the Lord o'th day: give me, great Mars,

Some token of thy pleasure.

[Here they fall on their faces as formerly, and there is heard

  clanging of Armor, with a short Thunder as the burst of a

Battaile,

  whereupon they all rise and bow to the Altar.]

O Great Corrector of enormous times,

Shaker of ore-rank States, thou grand decider

Of dustie and old tytles, that healst with blood

The earth when it is sicke, and curst the world

O'th pluresie of people; I doe take

Thy signes auspiciously, and in thy name

To my designe march boldly. Let us goe.

[Exeunt.]

[Enter Palamon and his Knights, with the former observance.]

PALAMON.

Our stars must glister with new fire, or be

To daie extinct; our argument is love,

Which if the goddesse of it grant, she gives

Victory too: then blend your spirits with mine,

You, whose free noblenesse doe make my cause

Your personall hazard; to the goddesse Venus

Commend we our proceeding, and implore

Her power unto our partie. [Here they kneele as formerly.]

Haile, Soveraigne Queene of secrets, who hast power

To call the feircest Tyrant from his rage,

And weepe unto a Girle; that ha'st the might,

Even with an ey-glance, to choke Marsis Drom

And turne th'allarme to whispers; that canst make

A Criple florish with his Crutch, and cure him

Before Apollo; that may'st force the King

To be his subjects vassaile, and induce

Stale gravitie to daunce; the pould Bachelour—

Whose youth, like wonton Boyes through Bonfyres,

Have skipt thy flame—at seaventy thou canst catch

And make him, to the scorne of his hoarse throate,

Abuse yong laies of love: what godlike power

Hast thou not power upon? To Phoebus thou

Add'st flames hotter then his; the heavenly fyres

Did scortch his mortall Son, thine him; the huntresse

All moyst and cold, some say, began to throw

Her Bow away, and sigh. Take to thy grace

Me, thy vowd Souldier, who doe beare thy yoke

As t'wer a wreath of Roses, yet is heavier

Then Lead it selfe, stings more than Nettles.

I have never beene foule mouthd against thy law,

Nev'r reveald secret, for I knew none—would not,

Had I kend all that were; I never practised

Vpon mans wife, nor would the Libells reade

Of liberall wits; I never at great feastes

Sought to betray a Beautie, but have blush'd

At simpring Sirs that did; I have beene harsh

To large Confessors, and have hotly ask'd them

If they had Mothers: I had one, a woman,

And women t'wer they wrong'd. I knew a man

Of eightie winters, this I told them, who

A Lasse of foureteene brided; twas thy power

To put life into dust; the aged Crampe

Had screw'd his square foote round,

The Gout had knit his fingers into knots,

Torturing Convulsions from his globie eyes,

Had almost drawne their spheeres, that what was life

In him seem'd torture: this Anatomie

Had by his yong faire pheare a Boy, and I

Beleev'd it was him, for she swore it was,

And who would not beleeve her? briefe, I am

To those that prate and have done no Companion;

To those that boast and have not a defyer;

To those that would and cannot a Rejoycer.

Yea, him I doe not love, that tells close offices

The fowlest way, nor names concealements in

The boldest language: such a one I am,

And vow that lover never yet made sigh

Truer then I. O, then, most soft, sweet goddesse,

Give me the victory of this question, which

Is true loves merit, and blesse me with a signe

Of thy great pleasure.

[Here Musicke is heard, Doves are seene to flutter; they fall

againe upon their faces, then on their knees.]

PALAMON.

O thou, that from eleven to ninetie raign'st

In mortall bosomes, whose chase is this world,

And we in heards thy game: I give thee thankes

For this faire Token, which, being layd unto

Mine innocent true heart, armes in assurance [They bow.]

My body to this businesse. Let us rise

And bow before the goddesse: Time comes on.

[Exeunt.]

[Still Musicke of Records.]

[Enter Emilia in white, her haire about her shoulders, (wearing) a wheaten wreath: One in white holding up her traine, her haire stucke with flowers: One before her carrying a silver Hynde, in which is conveyd Incense and sweet odours, which being set upon the Altar (of Diana) her maides standing a loofe, she sets fire to it; then they curtsey and kneele.]

EMILIA.

O sacred, shadowie, cold and constant Queene,

Abandoner of Revells, mute, contemplative,

Sweet, solitary, white as chaste, and pure

As windefand Snow, who to thy femall knights

Alow'st no more blood than will make a blush,

Which is their orders robe: I heere, thy Priest,

Am humbled fore thine Altar; O vouchsafe,

With that thy rare greene eye, which never yet

Beheld thing maculate, looke on thy virgin;

And, sacred silver Mistris, lend thine eare

(Which nev'r heard scurrill terme, into whose port

Ne're entred wanton found,) to my petition

Seasond with holy feare: This is my last

Of vestall office; I am bride habited,

But mayden harted, a husband I have pointed,

But doe not know him; out of two I should

Choose one and pray for his successe, but I

Am guiltlesse of election: of mine eyes,

Were I to loose one, they are equall precious,

I could doombe neither, that which perish'd should

Goe too't unsentenc'd: Therefore, most modest Queene,

He of the two Pretenders, that best loves me

And has the truest title in't, Let him

Take off my wheaten Gerland, or else grant

The fyle and qualitie I hold, I may

Continue in thy Band.

[Here the Hynde vanishes under the Altar: and in the place ascends

   a Rose Tree, having one Rose upon it.]

See what our Generall of Ebbs and Flowes

Out from the bowells of her holy Altar

With sacred act advances! But one Rose:

If well inspird, this Battaile shal confound

Both these brave Knights, and I, a virgin flowre

Must grow alone unpluck'd.

[Here is heard a sodaine twang of Instruments, and the Rose fals\

 from the Tree (which vanishes under the altar.)]

The flowre is falne, the Tree descends: O, Mistris,

Thou here dischargest me; I shall be gather'd:

I thinke so, but I know not thine owne will;

Vnclaspe thy Misterie.—I hope she's pleas'd,

Her Signes were gratious.

[They curtsey and Exeunt.]

SCENE 2. (A darkened Room in the Prison.)

[Enter Doctor, Iaylor and Wooer, in habite of Palamon.]

DOCTOR.

Has this advice I told you, done any good upon her?

WOOER.

O very much; The maids that kept her company

Have halfe perswaded her that I am Palamon;

Within this halfe houre she came smiling to me,

And asked me what I would eate, and when I would kisse her:

I told her presently, and kist her twice.

DOCTOR.

Twas well done; twentie times had bin far better,

For there the cure lies mainely.

WOOER.

Then she told me

She would watch with me to night, for well she knew

What houre my fit would take me.

DOCTOR.

Let her doe so,

And when your fit comes, fit her home,

And presently.

WOOER.

She would have me sing.

DOCTOR.

You did so?

WOOER.

No.

DOCTOR.

Twas very ill done, then;

You should observe her ev'ry way.

WOOER.

Alas,

I have no voice, Sir, to confirme her that way.

DOCTOR.

That's all one, if yee make a noyse;

If she intreate againe, doe any thing,—

Lye with her, if she aske you.

IAILOR.

Hoa, there, Doctor!

DOCTOR.

Yes, in the waie of cure.

IAILOR.

But first, by your leave,

I'th way of honestie.

DOCTOR.

That's but a nicenesse,

Nev'r cast your child away for honestie;

Cure her first this way, then if shee will be honest,

She has the path before her.

IAILOR.

Thanke yee, Doctor.

DOCTOR.

Pray, bring her in,

And let's see how shee is.

IAILOR.

I will, and tell her

Her Palamon staies for her: But, Doctor,

Me thinkes you are i'th wrong still.

[Exit Iaylor.]

DOCTOR.

Goe, goe:

You Fathers are fine Fooles: her honesty?

And we should give her physicke till we finde that—

WOOER.

Why, doe you thinke she is not honest, Sir?

DOCTOR.

How old is she?

WOOER.

She's eighteene.

DOCTOR.

She may be,

But that's all one; tis nothing to our purpose.

What ere her Father saies, if you perceave

Her moode inclining that way that I spoke of,

Videlicet, the way of flesh—you have me?

WOOER.

Yet, very well, Sir.

DOCTOR.

Please her appetite,

And doe it home; it cures her, ipso facto,

The mellencholly humour that infects her.

WOOER.

I am of your minde, Doctor.

               [Enter Iaylor, Daughter, Maide.]

DOCTOR.

You'l finde it so; she comes, pray humour her.

IAILOR.

Come, your Love Palamon staies for you, childe,

And has done this long houre, to visite you.

DAUGHTER.

I thanke him for his gentle patience;

He's a kind Gentleman, and I am much bound to him.

Did you nev'r see the horse he gave me?

IAILOR.

Yes.

DAUGHTER.

How doe you like him?

IAILOR.

He's a very faire one.

DAUGHTER.

You never saw him dance?

IAILOR.

No.

DAUGHTER.

I have often.

He daunces very finely, very comely,

And for a Iigge, come cut and long taile to him,

He turnes ye like a Top.

IAILOR.

That's fine, indeede.

DAUGHTER.

Hee'l dance the Morris twenty mile an houre,

And that will founder the best hobby-horse

(If I have any skill) in all the parish,

And gallops to the turne of LIGHT A' LOVE:

What thinke you of this horse?

IAILOR.

Having these vertues,

I thinke he might be broght to play at Tennis.

DAUGHTER.

Alas, that's nothing.

IAILOR.

Can he write and reade too?

DAUGHTER.

A very faire hand, and casts himselfe th'accounts

Of all his hay and provender: That Hostler

Must rise betime that cozens him. You know

The Chestnut Mare the Duke has?

IAILOR.

Very well.

DAUGHTER.

She is horribly in love with him, poore beast,

But he is like his master, coy and scornefull.

IAILOR.

What dowry has she?

DAUGHTER.

Some two hundred Bottles,

And twenty strike of Oates; but hee'l ne're have her;

He lispes in's neighing, able to entice

A Millars Mare: Hee'l be the death of her.

DOCTOR.

What stuffe she utters!

IAILOR.

Make curtsie; here your love comes.

WOOER.

Pretty soule,

How doe ye? that's a fine maide, ther's a curtsie!

DAUGHTER.

Yours to command ith way of honestie.

How far is't now to'th end o'th world, my Masters?

DOCTOR.

Why, a daies Iorney, wench.

DAUGHTER.

Will you goe with me?

WOOER.

What shall we doe there, wench?

DAUGHTER.

Why, play at stoole ball:

What is there else to doe?

WOOER.

I am content,

If we shall keepe our wedding there.

DAUGHTER.

Tis true:

For there, I will assure you, we shall finde

Some blind Priest for the purpose, that will venture

To marry us, for here they are nice, and foolish;

Besides, my father must be hang'd to morrow

And that would be a blot i'th businesse.

Are not you Palamon?

WOOER.

Doe not you know me?

DAUGHTER.

Yes, but you care not for me; I have nothing

But this pore petticoate, and too corse Smockes.

WOOER.

That's all one; I will have you.

DAUGHTER.

Will you surely?

WOOER.

Yes, by this faire hand, will I.

DAUGHTER.

Wee'l to bed, then.

WOOER.

Ev'n when you will. [Kisses her.]

DAUGHTER.

O Sir, you would faine be nibling.

WOOER.

Why doe you rub my kisse off?

DAUGHTER.

Tis a sweet one,

And will perfume me finely against the wedding.

Is not this your Cosen Arcite?

DOCTOR.

Yes, sweet heart,

And I am glad my Cosen Palamon

Has made so faire a choice.

DAUGHTER.

Doe you thinke hee'l have me?

DOCTOR.

Yes, without doubt.

DAUGHTER.

Doe you thinke so too?

IAILOR.

Yes.

DAUGHTER.

We shall have many children:—Lord, how y'ar growne!

My Palamon, I hope, will grow, too, finely,

Now he's at liberty: Alas, poore Chicken,

He was kept downe with hard meate and ill lodging,

But ile kisse him up againe.

[Enter a Messenger.]

MESSENGER.

What doe you here? you'l loose the noblest sight

That ev'r was seene.

IAILOR.

Are they i'th Field?

MESSENGER.

They are.

You beare a charge there too.

IAILOR.

Ile away straight.

I must ev'n leave you here.

DOCTOR.

Nay, wee'l goe with you;

I will not loose the Fight.

IAILOR.

How did you like her?

DOCTOR.

Ile warrant you, within these 3. or 4. daies

Ile make her right againe. You must not from her,

But still preserve her in this way.

WOOER.

I will.

DOCTOR.

Lets get her in.

WOOER.

Come, sweete, wee'l goe to dinner;

And then weele play at Cardes.

DAUGHTER.

And shall we kisse too?

WOOER.

A hundred times.

DAUGHTER.

And twenty.

WOOER.

I, and twenty.

DAUGHTER.

And then wee'l sleepe together.

DOCTOR.

Take her offer.

WOOER.

Yes, marry, will we.

DAUGHTER.

But you shall not hurt me.

WOOER.

I will not, sweete.

DAUGHTER.

If you doe, Love, ile cry.

[Florish. Exeunt]

SCENE 3. (A Place near the Lists.)

[Enter Theseus, Hipolita, Emilia, Perithous: and some Attendants, (T. Tucke: Curtis.)]

EMILIA.

Ile no step further.

PERITHOUS.

Will you loose this sight?

EMILIA.

I had rather see a wren hawke at a fly

Then this decision; ev'ry blow that falls

Threats a brave life, each stroake laments

The place whereon it fals, and sounds more like

A Bell then blade: I will stay here;

It is enough my hearing shall be punishd

With what shall happen—gainst the which there is

No deaffing, but to heare—not taint mine eye

With dread sights, it may shun.

PERITHOUS.

Sir, my good Lord,

Your Sister will no further.

THESEUS.

Oh, she must.

She shall see deeds of honour in their kinde,

Which sometime show well, pencild. Nature now

Shall make and act the Story, the beleife

Both seald with eye and eare; you must be present,

You are the victours meede, the price, and garlond

To crowne the Questions title.

EMILIA.

Pardon me;

If I were there, I'ld winke.

THESEUS.

You must be there;

This Tryall is as t'wer i'th night, and you

The onely star to shine.

EMILIA.

I am extinct;

There is but envy in that light, which showes

The one the other: darkenes, which ever was

The dam of horrour, who do's stand accurst

Of many mortall Millions, may even now,

By casting her blacke mantle over both,

That neither coulde finde other, get her selfe

Some part of a good name, and many a murther

Set off wherto she's guilty.

HIPPOLITA.

You must goe.

EMILIA.

In faith, I will not.

THESEUS.

Why, the knights must kindle

Their valour at your eye: know, of this war

You are the Treasure, and must needes be by

To give the Service pay.

EMILIA.

Sir, pardon me;

The tytle of a kingdome may be tride

Out of it selfe.

THESEUS.

Well, well, then, at your pleasure;

Those that remaine with you could wish their office

To any of their Enemies.

HIPPOLITA.

Farewell, Sister;

I am like to know your husband fore your selfe

By some small start of time: he whom the gods

Doe of the two know best, I pray them he

Be made your Lot.

[Exeunt Theseus, Hipolita, Perithous, &c.]

EMILIA.

Arcite is gently visagd; yet his eye

Is like an Engyn bent, or a sharpe weapon

In a soft sheath; mercy and manly courage

Are bedfellowes in his visage. Palamon

Has a most menacing aspect: his brow

Is grav'd, and seemes to bury what it frownes on;

Yet sometime tis not so, but alters to

The quallity of his thoughts; long time his eye

Will dwell upon his object. Mellencholly

Becomes him nobly; So do's Arcites mirth,

But Palamons sadnes is a kinde of mirth,

So mingled, as if mirth did make him sad,

And sadnes, merry; those darker humours that

Sticke misbecomingly on others, on them

Live in faire dwelling. [Cornets. Trompets sound as to a

charge.]

Harke, how yon spurs to spirit doe incite

The Princes to their proofe! Arcite may win me,

And yet may Palamon wound Arcite to

The spoyling of his figure. O, what pitty

Enough for such a chance; if I were by,

I might doe hurt, for they would glance their eies

Toward my Seat, and in that motion might

Omit a ward, or forfeit an offence

Which crav'd that very time: it is much better

I am not there; oh better never borne

Then minister to such harme. [Cornets. A great cry and noice within,

crying 'a Palamon'.] What is the chance?

[Enter Servant.]

SERVANT.

The Crie's 'a Palamon'.

EMILIA.

Then he has won! Twas ever likely;

He lookd all grace and successe, and he is

Doubtlesse the prim'st of men: I pre'thee, run

And tell me how it goes. [Showt, and Cornets: Crying, 'a

Palamon.']

SERVANT.

Still Palamon.

EMILIA.

Run and enquire. Poore Servant, thou hast lost;

Vpon my right side still I wore thy picture,

Palamons on the left: why so, I know not;

I had no end in't else, chance would have it so.

On the sinister side the heart lyes; Palamon

Had the best boding chance. [Another cry, and showt within, and

Cornets.] This burst of clamour

Is sure th'end o'th Combat.

[Enter Servant.]

SERVANT.

They saide that Palamon had Arcites body

Within an inch o'th Pyramid, that the cry

Was generall 'a Palamon': But, anon,

Th'Assistants made a brave redemption, and

The two bold Tytlers, at this instant are

Hand to hand at it.

EMILIA.

Were they metamorphisd

Both into one! oh why? there were no woman

Worth so composd a Man: their single share,

Their noblenes peculier to them, gives

The prejudice of disparity, values shortnes, [Cornets. Cry within,

Arcite, Arcite.]

To any Lady breathing—More exulting?

Palamon still?

SERVANT.

Nay, now the sound is Arcite.

EMILIA.

I pre'thee, lay attention to the Cry, [Cornets. A great showt and cry, 'Arcite, victory!'] Set both thine eares to'th busines.

SERVANT.

The cry is

'Arcite', and 'victory', harke: 'Arcite, victory!'

The Combats consummation is proclaim'd

By the wind Instruments.

EMILIA.

Halfe sights saw

That Arcite was no babe; god's lyd, his richnes

And costlines of spirit look't through him, it could

No more be hid in him then fire in flax,

Then humble banckes can goe to law with waters,

That drift windes force to raging: I did thinke

Good Palamon would miscarry; yet I knew not

Why I did thinke so; Our reasons are not prophets,

When oft our fancies are. They are comming off:

Alas, poore Palamon! [Cornets.]

[Enter Theseus, Hipolita, Pirithous, Arcite as victor, and attendants, &c.]

THESEUS.

Lo, where our Sister is in expectation,

Yet quaking, and unsetled.—Fairest Emily,

The gods by their divine arbitrament

Have given you this Knight; he is a good one

As ever strooke at head. Give me your hands;

Receive you her, you him; be plighted with

A love that growes, as you decay.

ARCITE.

Emily,

To buy you, I have lost what's deerest to me,

Save what is bought, and yet I purchase cheapely,

As I doe rate your value.

THESEUS.

O loved Sister,

He speakes now of as brave a Knight as ere

Did spur a noble Steed: Surely, the gods

Would have him die a Batchelour, least his race

Should shew i'th world too godlike: His behaviour

So charmed me, that me thought Alcides was

To him a sow of lead: if I could praise

Each part of him to'th all I have spoke, your Arcite

Did not loose by't; For he that was thus good

Encountred yet his Better. I have heard

Two emulous Philomels beate the eare o'th night

With their contentious throates, now one the higher,

Anon the other, then againe the first,

And by and by out breasted, that the sence

Could not be judge betweene 'em: So it far'd

Good space betweene these kinesmen; till heavens did

Make hardly one the winner. Weare the Girlond

With joy that you have won: For the subdude,

Give them our present Iustice, since I know

Their lives but pinch 'em; Let it here be done.

The Sceane's not for our seeing, goe we hence,

Right joyfull, with some sorrow.—Arme your prize,

I know you will not loose her.—Hipolita,

I see one eye of yours conceives a teare

The which it will deliver. [Florish.]

EMILIA.

Is this wynning?

Oh all you heavenly powers, where is your mercy?

But that your wils have saide it must be so,

And charge me live to comfort this unfriended,

This miserable Prince, that cuts away

A life more worthy from him then all women,

I should, and would, die too.

HIPPOLITA.

Infinite pitty,

That fowre such eies should be so fixd on one

That two must needes be blinde fort.

THESEUS.

So it is.

[Exeunt.]

SCENE 4. (The same; a Block prepared.)

[Enter Palamon and his Knightes pyniond: Iaylor, Executioner, &c. Gard.]

(PALAMON.)

Ther's many a man alive that hath out liv'd

The love o'th people; yea, i'th selfesame state

Stands many a Father with his childe; some comfort

We have by so considering: we expire

And not without mens pitty. To live still,

Have their good wishes; we prevent

The loathsome misery of age, beguile

The Gowt and Rheume, that in lag howres attend

For grey approachers; we come towards the gods

Yong and unwapper'd, not halting under Crymes

Many and stale: that sure shall please the gods,

Sooner than such, to give us Nectar with 'em,

For we are more cleare Spirits. My deare kinesmen,

Whose lives (for this poore comfort) are laid downe,

You have sould 'em too too cheape.

1. KNIGHT.

What ending could be

Of more content? ore us the victors have

Fortune, whose title is as momentary,

As to us death is certaine: A graine of honour

They not ore'-weigh us.

2. KNIGHT.

Let us bid farewell;

And with our patience anger tottring Fortune,

Who at her certain'st reeles.

3. KNIGHT.

Come; who begins?

PALAMON.

Ev'n he that led you to this Banket shall

Taste to you all.—Ah ha, my Friend, my Friend,

Your gentle daughter gave me freedome once;

You'l see't done now for ever: pray, how do'es she?

I heard she was not well; her kind of ill

Gave me some sorrow.

IAILOR.

Sir, she's well restor'd,

And to be married shortly.

PALAMON.

By my short life,

I am most glad on't; Tis the latest thing

I shall be glad of; pre'thee tell her so:

Commend me to her, and to peece her portion,

Tender her this. [Gives purse.]

1. KNIGHT.

Nay lets be offerers all.

2. KNIGHT.

Is it a maide?

PALAMON.

Verily, I thinke so,

A right good creature, more to me deserving

Then I can quight or speake of.

ALL KNIGHTS.

Commend us to her. [They give their purses.]

IAILOR.

The gods requight you all,

And make her thankefull.

PALAMON.

Adiew; and let my life be now as short,

As my leave taking. [Lies on the Blocke.]

1. KNIGHT.

Leade, couragious Cosin.

2. KNIGHT.

Wee'l follow cheerefully. [A great noise within crying, 'run, save, hold!']

[Enter in hast a Messenger.]

MESSENGER.

Hold, hold! O hold, hold, hold!

[**Enter Pirithous in haste.**]

PERITHOUS.

Hold! hoa! It is a cursed hast you made,

If you have done so quickly. Noble Palamon,

The gods will shew their glory in a life,

That thou art yet to leade.

PALAMON.

Can that be,

When Venus, I have said, is false? How doe things fare?

PERITHOUS.

Arise, great Sir, and give the tydings eare

That are most dearly sweet and bitter.

PALAMON.

What

Hath wakt us from our dreame?

PERITHOUS.

List then: your Cosen,

Mounted upon a Steed that Emily

Did first bestow on him, a blacke one, owing

Not a hayre worth of white—which some will say

Weakens his price, and many will not buy

His goodnesse with this note: Which superstition

Heere findes allowance—On this horse is Arcite

Trotting the stones of Athens, which the Calkins

Did rather tell then trample; for the horse

Would make his length a mile, if't pleas'd his Rider

To put pride in him: as he thus went counting

The flinty pavement, dancing, as t'wer, to'th Musicke

His owne hoofes made; (for as they say from iron

Came Musickes origen) what envious Flint,

Cold as old Saturne, and like him possest

With fire malevolent, darted a Sparke,

Or what feirce sulphur else, to this end made,

I comment not;—the hot horse, hot as fire,

Tooke Toy at this, and fell to what disorder

His power could give his will; bounds, comes on end,

Forgets schoole dooing, being therein traind,

And of kind mannadge; pig-like he whines

At the sharpe Rowell, which he freats at rather

Then any jot obaies; seekes all foule meanes

Of boystrous and rough Iadrie, to dis-seate

His Lord, that kept it bravely: when nought serv'd,

When neither Curb would cracke, girth breake nor diffring plunges

Dis-roote his Rider whence he grew, but that

He kept him tweene his legges, on his hind hoofes on end he stands,

That Arcites leggs, being higher then his head,

Seem'd with strange art to hand: His victors wreath

Even then fell off his head: and presently

Backeward the Iade comes ore, and his full poyze

Becomes the Riders loade: yet is he living,

But such a vessell tis, that floates but for

The surge that next approaches: he much desires

To have some speech with you: Loe he appeares.

    [Enter Theseus, Hipolita, Emilia, Arcite in a chaire.]

PALAMON.

O miserable end of our alliance!

The gods are mightie, Arcite: if thy heart,

Thy worthie, manly heart, be yet unbroken,

Give me thy last words; I am Palamon,

One that yet loves thee dying.

ARCITE.

Take Emilia

And with her all the worlds joy: Reach thy hand:

Farewell: I have told my last houre. I was false,

Yet never treacherous: Forgive me, Cosen:—

One kisse from faire Emilia: Tis done:

Take her: I die.

PALAMON.

Thy brave soule seeke Elizium.

EMILIA.

Ile close thine eyes, Prince; blessed soules be with thee!

Thou art a right good man, and while I live,

This day I give to teares.

PALAMON.

And I to honour.

THESEUS.

In this place first you fought: ev'n very here

I sundred you: acknowledge to the gods

Our thankes that you are living.

His part is playd, and though it were too short,

He did it well: your day is lengthned, and

The blissefull dew of heaven do's arowze you.

The powerfull Venus well hath grac'd her Altar,

And given you your love: Our Master Mars

Hath vouch'd his Oracle, and to Arcite gave

The grace of the Contention: So the Deities

Have shewd due justice: Beare this hence.

PALAMON.

O Cosen,

That we should things desire, which doe cost us

The losse of our desire! That nought could buy

Deare love, but losse of deare love!

THESEUS.

Never Fortune

Did play a subtler Game: The conquerd triumphes,

The victor has the Losse: yet in the passage

The gods have beene most equall: Palamon,

Your kinseman hath confest the right o'th Lady

Did lye in you, for you first saw her, and

Even then proclaimd your fancie: He restord her

As your stolne Iewell, and desir'd your spirit

To send him hence forgiven; The gods my justice

Take from my hand, and they themselves become

The Executioners: Leade your Lady off;

And call your Lovers from the stage of death,

Whom I adopt my Frinds. A day or two

Let us looke sadly, and give grace unto

The Funerall of Arcite; in whose end

The visages of Bridegroomes weele put on

And smile with Palamon; for whom an houre,

But one houre, since, I was as dearely sorry,

As glad of Arcite: and am now as glad,

As for him sorry. O you heavenly Charmers,

What things you make of us! For what we lacke

We laugh, for what we have, are sorry: still

Are children in some kind. Let us be thankefull

For that which is, and with you leave dispute

That are above our question. Let's goe off,

And beare us like the time.

[Florish. Exeunt.]

EPILOGUE

I would now aske ye how ye like the Play,

But, as it is with Schoole Boyes, cannot say,

I am cruell fearefull: pray, yet stay a while,

And let me looke upon ye: No man smile?

Then it goes hard, I see; He that has

Lov'd a yong hansome wench, then, show his face—

Tis strange if none be heere—and if he will

Against his Conscience, let him hisse, and kill

Our Market: Tis in vaine, I see, to stay yee;

Have at the worst can come, then! Now what say ye?

And yet mistake me not: I am not bold;

We have no such cause. If the tale we have told

(For tis no other) any way content ye

(For to that honest purpose it was ment ye)

We have our end; and ye shall have ere long,

I dare say, many a better, to prolong

Your old loves to us: we, and all our might

Rest at your service. Gentlemen, good night.

[Florish.]

FINISH

About Author

Shakespeare produced most of his known works between 1589 and 1613. His early plays were primarily comedies and histories and are regarded as some of the best work produced in these genres. Until about 1608, he wrote mainly tragedies, among them Hamlet, Othello, King Lear, and Macbeth, all considered to be among the finest works in the English language. In the last phase of his life, he wrote tragicomedies (also known as romances) and collaborated with other playwrights.

Many of Shakespeare's plays were published in editions of varying quality and accuracy in his lifetime. However, in 1623, two fellow actors and friends of Shakespeare's, John Heminges and Henry Condell, published a more definitive text known as the First Folio, a posthumous collected edition of Shakespeare's dramatic works that included all but two of his plays. The volume was prefaced with a poem by Ben Jonson, in which Jonson presciently hails Shakespeare in a now-famous quote as "not of an age, but for all time".

Throughout the 20th and 21st centuries, Shakespeare's works have been continually adapted and rediscovered by new movements in scholarship and performance. His plays remain popular and are studied, performed, and reinterpreted through various cultural and political contexts around the world.

Early life

William Shakespeare was the son of John Shakespeare, an alderman and a successful glover (glove-maker) originally from Snitterfield, and Mary Arden, the daughter of an affluent landowning farmer. He was born in Stratford-upon-Avon and baptised there on 26 April 1564. His actual date of birth remains unknown, but is traditionally observed on 23 April, Saint George's Day. This date, which can be traced to a mistake made by an 18th-century scholar, has proved appealing to biographers because Shakespeare died on the same date in 1616. He was the third of eight children, and the eldest surviving son.

Although no attendance records for the period survive, most biographers agree that Shakespeare was probably educated at the King's New School in Stratford, a free school chartered in 1553, about a quarter-mile (400 m) from his home. Grammar schools varied in quality during the Elizabethan era, but grammar school curricula were largely similar: the basic Latin text was standardised by royal decree, and the school would have provided an intensive education in grammar based upon Latin classical authors.

At the age of 18, Shakespeare married 26-year-old Anne Hathaway. The consistory court of the Diocese of Worcester issued a marriage licence on 27 November 1582. The next day, two of Hathaway's neighbours posted bonds guaranteeing that no lawful claims impeded the marriage. The ceremony may have been arranged in some haste since the Worcester chancellor allowed the marriage banns to be read once instead of the usual three times, and six months after the marriage Anne gave birth to a daughter, Susanna, baptised 26 May 1583. Twins, son Hamnet and daughter Judith, followed almost two years later and were baptised 2 February 1585. Hamnet died of unknown causes at the age of 11 and was buried 11 August 1596.

After the birth of the twins, Shakespeare left few historical traces until he is mentioned as part of the London theatre scene in 1592. The exception is the appearance of his name in the "complaints bill" of a law case before the Queen's Bench court at Westminster dated Michaelmas Term 1588 and 9 October 1589. Scholars refer to the years between 1585 and 1592 as Shakespeare's "lost years". Biographers attempting to account for this period have reported many apocryphal stories. Nicholas Rowe, Shakespeare's first biographer, recounted a Stratford legend that Shakespeare fled the town for London to escape prosecution for deer poaching in the estate of local squire Thomas Lucy. Shakespeare is also supposed to have taken his revenge on Lucy by writing a scurrilous ballad about him. Another 18th-century story has Shakespeare starting his theatrical career minding the horses of theatre patrons in London. John Aubrey reported that Shakespeare had been a country schoolmaster. Some 20th-century scholars have suggested that Shakespeare may have been employed as a schoolmaster by Alexander

Hoghton of Lancashire, a Catholic landowner who named a certain "William Shakeshafte" in his will. Little evidence substantiates such stories other than hearsay collected after his death, and Shakeshafte was a common name in the Lancashire area.

London and theatrical career

It is not known definitively when Shakespeare began writing, but contemporary allusions and records of performances show that several of his plays were on the London stage by 1592. By then, he was sufficiently known in London to be attacked in print by the playwright Robert Greene in his Groats-Worth of Wit:

... there is an upstart Crow, beautified with our feathers, that with his Tiger's heart wrapped in a Player's hide, supposes he is as well able to bombast out a blank verse as the best of you: and being an absolute Johannes factotum, is in his own conceit the only Shake-scene in a country.

Scholars differ on the exact meaning of Greene's words, but most agree that Greene was accusing Shakespeare of reaching above his rank in trying to match such university-educated writers as Christopher Marlowe, Thomas Nashe, and Greene himself (the so-called "University Wits"). The italicised phrase parodying the line "Oh, tiger's heart wrapped in a woman's hide" from Shakespeare's Henry VI, Part 3, along with the pun "Shake-scene", clearly identify Shakespeare as Greene's target. As used here, Johannes Factotum ("Jack of all trades") refers to a second-rate tinkerer with the work of others, rather than the more common "universal genius".

Greene's attack is the earliest surviving mention of Shakespeare's work in the theatre. Biographers suggest that his career may have begun any time from the mid-1580s to just before Greene's remarks. After 1594, Shakespeare's plays were performed only by the Lord Chamberlain's Men, a company owned by a group of players, including Shakespeare, that soon became the leading playing company in London. After the death of Queen Elizabeth in 1603, the company was awarded a royal patent by the new King James I, and changed its name to the King's Men.

"All the world's a stage,

and all the men and women merely players:

they have their exits and their entrances;

and one man in his time plays many parts ..."

—As You Like It, Act II, Scene 7, 139–142

In 1599, a partnership of members of the company built their own theatre on the south bank of the River Thames, which they named the Globe. In 1608, the partnership also took over the Blackfriars indoor theatre. Extant records of Shakespeare's property purchases and investments indicate that his association with the company made him a wealthy man, and in 1597, he bought the second-largest house in Stratford, New Place, and in 1605, invested in a share of the parish tithes in Stratford.

Some of Shakespeare's plays were published in quarto editions, beginning in 1594, and by 1598, his name had become a selling point and began to appear on the title pages. Shakespeare continued to act in his own and other plays after his success as a playwright. The 1616 edition of Ben Jonson's Works names him on the cast lists for Every Man in His Humour (1598) and Sejanus His Fall (1603). The absence of his name from the 1605 cast list for Jonson's Volpone is taken by some scholars as a sign that his acting career was nearing its end. The First Folio of 1623, however, lists Shakespeare as one of "the Principal Actors in all these Plays", some of which were first staged after Volpone, although we cannot know for certain which roles he played. In 1610, John Davies of Hereford wrote that "good Will" played "kingly" roles. In 1709, Rowe passed down a tradition that Shakespeare played the ghost of Hamlet's father. Later traditions maintain that he also played Adam in As You Like It, and the Chorus in Henry V, though scholars doubt the sources of that information.

Throughout his career, Shakespeare divided his time between London and Stratford. In 1596, the year before he bought New Place as his family home in Stratford, Shakespeare was living in the parish of St. Helen's, Bishopsgate, north of the River Thames. He moved across the river to Southwark by 1599, the same year his company constructed the Globe Theatre there. By 1604, he had moved north of the river again, to an area north of St Paul's Cathedral with many fine houses. There, he rented rooms from a French Huguenot named Christopher Mountjoy, a maker of ladies' wigs and other headgear.

Later years and death

Rowe was the first biographer to record the tradition, repeated by Johnson, that Shakespeare retired to Stratford "some years before his death". He was still working as an actor in London in 1608; in an answer to the sharers' petition in 1635, Cuthbert Burbage stated that after purchasing the lease of the Blackfriars Theatre in 1608 from Henry Evans, the King's Men "placed men players" there, "which were Heminges, Condell, Shakespeare, etc.". However, it is perhaps relevant that the bubonic plague raged in London throughout 1609. The London public playhouses were repeatedly closed during extended outbreaks of the plague (a total of over 60 months closure between May 1603 and February 1610), which meant there was often no acting work. Retirement from all work was uncommon at that time. Shakespeare continued to visit London during the years 1611–1614. In 1612, he was called as a witness in Bellott v. Mountjoy, a court case concerning the marriage settlement of Mountjoy's daughter, Mary. In March 1613, he bought a gatehouse in the former Blackfriars priory; and from November 1614, he was in London for several weeks with his son-in-law, John Hall. After 1610, Shakespeare wrote fewer plays, and none are attributed to him after 1613. His last three plays were collaborations, probably with John Fletcher, who succeeded him as the house playwright of the King's Men.

Shakespeare died on 23 April 1616, at the age of 52. He died within a month of signing his will, a document which he begins by describing himself as being in "perfect health". No extant contemporary source explains how or why he died. Half a century later, John Ward, the vicar of Stratford, wrote in his notebook: "Shakespeare, Drayton, and Ben Jonson had a merry meeting and, it seems, drank too hard, for Shakespeare died of a fever there contracted", not an impossible scenario since Shakespeare knew Jonson and Drayton. Of the tributes from fellow authors, one refers to his relatively sudden death: "We wondered, Shakespeare, that thou went'st so soon / From

209

the world's stage to the grave's tiring room."

He was survived by his wife and two daughters. Susanna had married a physician, John Hall, in 1607, and Judith had married Thomas Quiney, a vintner, two months before Shakespeare's death. Shakespeare signed his last will and testament on 25 March 1616; the following day, his new son-in-law, Thomas Quiney was found guilty of fathering an illegitimate son by Margaret Wheeler, who had died during childbirth. Thomas was ordered by the church court to do public penance, which would have caused much shame and embarrassment for the Shakespeare family.

Shakespeare bequeathed the bulk of his large estate to his elder daughter Susanna under stipulations that she pass it down intact to "the first son of her body". The Quineys had three children, all of whom died without marrying. The Halls had one child, Elizabeth, who married twice but died without children in 1670, ending Shakespeare's direct line. Shakespeare's will scarcely mentions his wife, Anne, who was probably entitled to one-third of his estate automatically. He did make a point, however, of leaving her "my second best bed", a bequest that has led to much speculation. Some scholars see the bequest as an insult to Anne, whereas others believe that the second-best bed would have been the matrimonial bed and therefore rich in significance.

Shakespeare was buried in the chancel of the Holy Trinity Church two days after his death. The epitaph carved into the stone slab covering his grave includes a curse against moving his bones, which was carefully avoided during restoration of the church in 2008:

Good frend for Iesvs sake forbeare,

To digg the dvst encloased heare.

Bleste be Middle English the.svg man Middle English that.svg spares thes stones,

And cvrst be he Middle English that.svg moves my bones.

(Modern spelling: Good friend, for Jesus' sake forbear, / To dig the dust enclosed here. / Blessed be the man that spares these stones, / And cursed be he that moves my bones.)

Some time before 1623, a funerary monument was erected in his memory on the north wall, with a half-effigy of him in the act of writing. Its plaque compares him to Nestor, Socrates, and Virgil. In 1623, in conjunction with the publication of the First Folio, the Droeshout engraving was published.

Shakespeare has been commemorated in many statues and memorials around the world, including funeral monuments in Southwark Cathedral and Poets' Corner in Westminster Abbey.

Plays

Most playwrights of the period typically collaborated with others at some point, and critics agree that Shakespeare did the same, mostly early and late in his career. Some attributions, such as Titus Andronicus and the early history plays, remain controversial while The Two Noble Kinsmen and the lost Cardenio have well-attested contemporary documentation. Textual evidence also supports the view that several of the plays were revised by other writers after their original composition.

The first recorded works of Shakespeare are Richard III and the three parts of Henry VI, written in the early 1590s during a vogue for historical drama. Shakespeare's plays are difficult to date precisely, however, and studies of the texts suggest that Titus Andronicus, The Comedy of Errors, The Taming of the Shrew, and The Two Gentlemen of Verona may also belong to Shakespeare's earliest period. His first histories, which draw heavily on the 1587 edition of Raphael Holinshed's Chronicles of England, Scotland, and Ireland, dramatise the destructive results of weak or corrupt rule and have been interpreted as a justification for the origins of the Tudor dynasty. The early plays were influenced by the works of other Elizabethan dramatists, especially Thomas Kyd and Christopher Marlowe, by the traditions of medieval drama, and by the plays of Seneca. The Comedy of Errors was also based on classical models, but no source for The Taming of the Shrew has been found, though it is related to a separate play of the same name and may have derived from a folk story. Like The Two Gentlemen of Verona, in which two friends appear to approve of rape, the Shrew's story of the taming of a woman's independent

211

spirit by a man sometimes troubles modern critics, directors, and audiences.

Shakespeare's early classical and Italianate comedies, containing tight double plots and precise comic sequences, give way in the mid-1590s to the romantic atmosphere of his most acclaimed comedies. A Midsummer Night's Dream is a witty mixture of romance, fairy magic, and comic lowlife scenes. Shakespeare's next comedy, the equally romantic Merchant of Venice, contains a portrayal of the vengeful Jewish moneylender Shylock, which reflects Elizabethan views but may appear derogatory to modern audiences. The wit and wordplay of Much Ado About Nothing, the charming rural setting of As You Like It, and the lively merrymaking of Twelfth Night complete Shakespeare's sequence of great comedies. After the lyrical Richard II, written almost entirely in verse, Shakespeare introduced prose comedy into the histories of the late 1590s, Henry IV, parts 1 and 2, and Henry V. His characters become more complex and tender as he switches deftly between comic and serious scenes, prose and poetry, and achieves the narrative variety of his mature work. This period begins and ends with two tragedies: Romeo and Juliet, the famous romantic tragedy of sexually charged adolescence, love, and death; and Julius Caesar—based on Sir Thomas North's 1579 translation of Plutarch's Parallel Lives—which introduced a new kind of drama. According to Shakespearean scholar James Shapiro, in Julius Caesar, "the various strands of politics, character, inwardness, contemporary events, even Shakespeare's own reflections on the act of writing, began to infuse each other".

In the early 17th century, Shakespeare wrote the so-called "problem plays" Measure for Measure, Troilus and Cressida, and All's Well That Ends Well and a number of his best known tragedies. Many critics believe that Shakespeare's greatest tragedies represent the peak of his art. The titular hero of one of Shakespeare's greatest tragedies, Hamlet, has probably been discussed more than any other Shakespearean character, especially for his famous soliloquy which begins "To be or not to be; that is the question". Unlike the introverted Hamlet, whose fatal flaw is hesitation, the heroes of the tragedies that followed, Othello and King Lear, are undone by hasty errors of judgement. The plots of Shakespeare's tragedies often hinge on such fatal errors or flaws, which overturn order and destroy the hero and those he loves. In Othello, the villain Iago stokes Othello's sexual jealousy to the point where he murders the innocent wife who loves him. In King Lear, the old king commits the tragic error of giving up his powers, initiating the events which lead to the torture and blinding of the Earl of Gloucester and the murder of Lear's youngest daughter Cordelia. According to the critic Frank Kermode, "the play-offers neither its good characters nor its audience any relief from its cruelty". In Macbeth, the shortest and most compressed of Shakespeare's tragedies, uncontrollable ambition incites Macbeth and his wife, Lady Macbeth, to murder the rightful king and usurp the throne until their own guilt destroys them in turn. In this play, Shakespeare adds a supernatural element to the tragic structure. His last major tragedies, Antony and Cleopatra and Coriolanus, contain some of Shakespeare's finest poetry and were considered his most successful tragedies by the poet and critic T.S. Eliot.

In his final period, Shakespeare turned to romance or tragicomedy and completed three more major plays: Cymbeline, The Winter's Tale, and The Tempest, as well as the collaboration, Pericles, Prince of Tyre. Less bleak than the tragedies, these four plays are graver in tone than the comedies of the 1590s, but they end with reconciliation and the forgiveness of potentially tragic errors. Some commentators have seen this change in mood as evidence of a more serene view of life on Shakespeare's part, but it may merely reflect the theatrical fashion of the day. Shakespeare collaborated on two further surviving plays, Henry VIII and The Two Noble Kinsmen, probably with John Fletcher.

Performances

It is not clear for which companies Shakespeare wrote his early plays. The title page of the 1594 edition of Titus Andronicus reveals that the play had been acted by three different troupes. After the plagues of 1592–3, Shakespeare's plays were performed by his own company at The Theatre and the Curtain in Shoreditch, north of the Thames. Londoners flocked there to see the first part of Henry IV, Leonard Digges recording, "Let but Falstaff come, Hal, Poins, the rest ... and you scarce shall have a room". When the company found themselves in dispute with their landlord, they pulled The

213

Theatre down and used the timbers to construct the Globe Theatre, the first playhouse built by actors for actors, on the south bank of the Thames at Southwark. The Globe opened in autumn 1599, with Julius Caesar one of the first plays staged. Most of Shakespeare's greatest post-1599 plays were written for the Globe, including Hamlet, Othello, and King Lear.

After the Lord Chamberlain's Men were renamed the King's Men in 1603, they entered a special relationship with the new King James. Although the performance records are patchy, the King's Men performed seven of Shakespeare's plays at court between 1 November 1604, and 31 October 1605, including two performances of The Merchant of Venice. After 1608, they performed at the indoor Blackfriars Theatre during the winter and the Globe during the summer. The indoor setting, combined with the Jacobean fashion for lavishly staged masques, allowed Shakespeare to introduce more elaborate stage devices. In Cymbeline, for example, Jupiter descends "in thunder and lightning, sitting upon an eagle: he throws a thunderbolt. The ghosts fall on their knees."

The actors in Shakespeare's company included the famous Richard Burbage, William Kempe, Henry Condell and John Heminges. Burbage played the leading role in the first performances of many of Shakespeare's plays, including Richard III, Hamlet, Othello, and King Lear. The popular comic actor Will Kempe played the servant Peter in Romeo and Juliet and Dogberry in Much Ado About Nothing, among other characters. He was replaced around 1600 by Robert Armin, who played roles such as Touchstone in As You Like It and the fool in King Lear. In 1613, Sir Henry Wotton recorded that Henry VIII "was set forth with many extraordinary circumstances of pomp and ceremony". On 29 June, however, a cannon set fire to the thatch of the Globe and burned the theatre to the ground, an event which pinpoints the date of a Shakespeare play with rare precision.

Textual sources

In 1623, John Heminges and Henry Condell, two of Shakespeare's friends from the King's Men, published the First Folio, a collected edition of Shakespeare's plays. It contained 36 texts, including 18 printed for the first time. Many of the plays had already appeared in quarto versions—flimsy books made from sheets of paper folded twice to make four leaves. No evidence suggests that Shakespeare approved these editions, which the First Folio describes as "stol'n and surreptitious copies". Nor did Shakespeare plan or expect his works to survive in any form at all; those works likely would have faded into oblivion but for his friends' spontaneous idea, after his death, to create and publish the First Folio.

Alfred Pollard termed some of the pre-1623 versions as "bad quartos" because of their adapted, paraphrased or garbled texts, which may in places have been reconstructed from memory. Where several versions of a play survive, each differs from the other. The differences may stem from copying or printing errors, from notes by actors or audience members, or from Shakespeare's own papers. In some cases, for example, Hamlet, Troilus and Cressida, and Othello, Shakespeare could have revised the texts between the quarto and folio editions. In the case of King Lear, however, while most modern editions do conflate them, the 1623 folio version is so different from the 1608 quarto that the Oxford Shakespeare prints them both, arguing that they cannot be conflated without confusion.

Influence from neighbours in London

Ten years of research by Geoffrey Marsh (museum director) of the Victoria and Albert Museum in London may have shown that Shakespeare got many of the ideas and information for his plays, from his neighbours that he lived near in London in the late 1590s.

Geoffrey Marsh found the site of Shakespeare's house in St Helen's Church, Bishopsgate parish, at the corner of St.Helen's churchyard and Bishopsgate Street, north of the churchyard, from the records of the Leathersellers Company. Many wealthy and notable people (including Sir John Spencer and Dr. Edward Jorden and Dr. Peter Turner), with connections across Europe, lived near Shakespeare.

Poems

In 1593 and 1594, when the theatres were closed because of plague,

Shakespeare published two narrative poems on sexual themes, Venus and Adonis and The Rape of Lucrece. He dedicated them to Henry Wriothesley, Earl of Southampton. In Venus and Adonis, an innocent Adonis rejects the sexual advances of Venus; while in The Rape of Lucrece, the virtuous wife Lucrece is raped by the lustful Tarquin. Influenced by Ovid's Metamorphoses, the poems show the guilt and moral confusion that result from uncontrolled lust. Both proved popular and were often reprinted during Shakespeare's lifetime. A third narrative poem, A Lover's Complaint, in which a young woman laments her seduction by a persuasive suitor, was printed in the first edition of the Sonnets in 1609. Most scholars now accept that Shakespeare wrote A Lover's Complaint. Critics consider that its fine qualities are marred by leaden effects. The Phoenix and the Turtle, printed in Robert Chester's 1601 Love's Martyr, mourns the deaths of the legendary phoenix and his lover, the faithful turtle dove. In 1599, two early drafts of sonnets 138 and 144 appeared in The Passionate Pilgrim, published under Shakespeare's name but without his permission.

Sonnets

Published in 1609, the Sonnets were the last of Shakespeare's non-dramatic works to be printed. Scholars are not certain when each of the 154 sonnets was composed, but evidence suggests that Shakespeare wrote sonnets throughout his career for a private readership. Even before the two unauthorised sonnets appeared in The Passionate Pilgrim in 1599, Francis Meres had referred in 1598 to Shakespeare's "sugred Sonnets among his private friends". Few analysts believe that the published collection follows Shakespeare's intended sequence. He seems to have planned two contrasting series: one about uncontrollable lust for a married woman of dark complexion (the "dark lady"), and one about conflicted love for a fair young man (the "fair youth"). It remains unclear if these figures represent real individuals, or if the authorial "I" who addresses them represents Shakespeare himself, though Wordsworth believed that with the sonnets "Shakespeare unlocked his heart".

"Shall I compare thee to a summer's day?

Thou art more lovely and more temperate ..."

—Lines from Shakespeare's Sonnet 18.

The 1609 edition was dedicated to a "Mr. W.H.", credited as "the only begetter" of the poems. It is not known whether this was written by Shakespeare himself or by the publisher, Thomas Thorpe, whose initials appear at the foot of the dedication page; nor is it known who Mr. W.H. was, despite numerous theories, or whether Shakespeare even authorised the publication. Critics praise the Sonnets as a profound meditation on the nature of love, sexual passion, procreation, death, and time.

Style

Shakespeare's first plays were written in the conventional style of the day. He wrote them in a stylised language that does not always spring naturally from the needs of the characters or the drama. The poetry depends on extended, sometimes elaborate metaphors and conceits, and the language is often rhetorical—written for actors to declaim rather than speak. The grand speeches in Titus Andronicus, in the view of some critics, often hold up the action, for example; and the verse in The Two Gentlemen of Verona has been described as stilted.

However, Shakespeare soon began to adapt the traditional styles to his own purposes. The opening soliloquy of Richard III has its roots in the self-declaration of Vice in medieval drama. At the same time, Richard's vivid self-awareness looks forward to the soliloquies of Shakespeare's mature plays. No single play marks a change from the traditional to the freer style. Shakespeare combined the two throughout his career, with Romeo and Juliet perhaps the best example of the mixing of the styles. By the time of Romeo and Juliet, Richard II, and A Midsummer Night's Dream in the mid-1590s, Shakespeare had begun to write a more natural poetry. He increasingly tuned his metaphors and images to the needs of the drama itself.

Shakespeare's standard poetic form was blank verse, composed in iambic pentameter. In practice, this meant that his verse was usually unrhymed and consisted of ten syllables to a line, spoken with a stress on every second syllable. The blank verse of his early plays is quite different from that of his later ones. It is often beautiful, but its sentences tend to start, pause, and finish at the end of lines, with the risk of monotony. Once Shakespeare mastered traditional blank verse, he began to interrupt and vary its flow. This technique releases the new power and flexibility of the poetry in plays such as Julius Caesar and Hamlet. Shakespeare uses it, for example, to convey the turmoil in Hamlet's mind:

> Sir, in my heart there was a kind of fighting
>
> That would not let me sleep. Methought I lay
>
> Worse than the mutines in the bilboes. Rashly—
>
> And prais'd be rashness for it—let us know
>
> Our indiscretion sometimes serves us well ...
>
> —Hamlet, Act 5, Scene 2, 4–8

After Hamlet, Shakespeare varied his poetic style further, particularly in the more emotional passages of the late tragedies. The literary critic A. C. Bradley described this style as "more concentrated, rapid, varied, and, in construction, less regular, not seldom twisted or elliptical". In the last phase of his career, Shakespeare adopted many techniques to achieve these effects. These included run-on lines, irregular pauses and stops, and extreme variations in sentence structure and length. In Macbeth, for example, the language darts from one unrelated metaphor or simile to another: "was the hope drunk/ Wherein you dressed yourself?" (1.7.35–38); "... pity, like a naked new-born babe/ Striding the blast, or heaven's cherubim, hors'd/ Upon the sightless couriers of the air ..." (1.7.21–25). The listener is challenged to complete the sense. The late romances, with their shifts in time and surprising turns of plot, inspired a last poetic style in which long and short sentences are set against one another, clauses are piled up, subject and object are reversed, and words are omitted, creating an effect of spontaneity.

Shakespeare combined poetic genius with a practical sense of the theatre. Like all playwrights of the time, he dramatised stories from sources such as Plutarch and Holinshed. He reshaped each plot to create several centres of interest and to show as many sides of a narrative to the audience as possible. This strength of design ensures that a Shakespeare play can survive translation, cutting and wide interpretation without loss to its core drama. As Shakespeare's mastery grew, he gave his characters clearer and more varied motivations and distinctive patterns of speech. He preserved aspects of his earlier style in the later plays, however. In Shakespeare's late romances, he deliberately returned to a more artificial style, which emphasised the illusion of theatre.

Influence

Shakespeare's work has made a lasting impression on later theatre and literature. In particular, he expanded the dramatic potential of characterisation, plot, language, and genre. Until Romeo and Juliet, for example, romance had not been viewed as a worthy topic for tragedy. Soliloquies had been used mainly to convey information about characters or events, but Shakespeare used them to explore characters' minds. His work heavily influenced later poetry. The Romantic poets attempted to revive Shakespearean verse drama, though with little success. Critic George Steiner described all English verse dramas from Coleridge to Tennyson as "feeble variations on Shakespearean themes."

Shakespeare influenced novelists such as Thomas Hardy, William Faulkner, and Charles Dickens. The American novelist Herman Melville's soliloquies owe much to Shakespeare; his Captain Ahab in Moby-Dick is a classic tragic hero, inspired by King Lear. Scholars have identified 20,000 pieces of music linked to Shakespeare's works. These include three operas by Giuseppe Verdi, Macbeth, Otello and Falstaff, whose critical standing compares with that of the source plays. Shakespeare has also inspired many painters, including the Romantics and the Pre-Raphaelites. The Swiss Romantic artist Henry Fuseli, a friend of William Blake, even translated Macbeth into German. The psychoanalyst Sigmund Freud drew on Shakespearean psychology, in particular, that of Hamlet, for his theories of human nature.

In Shakespeare's day, English grammar, spelling, and pronunciation were less standardised than they are now, and his use of language helped shape

219

modern English. Samuel Johnson quoted him more often than any other author in his A Dictionary of the English Language, the first serious work of its type. Expressions such as "with bated breath" (Merchant of Venice) and "a foregone conclusion" (Othello) have found their way into everyday English speech.

Works

Classification of the plays

Shakespeare's works include the 36 plays printed in the First Folio of 1623, listed according to their folio classification as comedies, histories, and tragedies. Two plays not included in the First Folio, The Two Noble Kinsmen and Pericles, Prince of Tyre, are now accepted as part of the canon, with today's scholars agreeing that Shakespeare made major contributions to the writing of both. No Shakespearean poems were included in the First Folio.

In the late 19th century, Edward Dowden classified four of the late comedies as romances, and though many scholars prefer to call them tragicomedies, Dowden's term is often used. In 1896, Frederick S. Boas coined the term "problem plays" to describe four plays: All's Well That Ends Well, Measure for Measure, Troilus and Cressida, and Hamlet. "Dramas as singular in theme and temper cannot be strictly called comedies or tragedies", he wrote. "We may, therefore, borrow a convenient phrase from the theatre of today and class them together as Shakespeare's problem plays." The term, much debated and sometimes applied to other plays, remains in use, though Hamlet is definitively classed as a tragedy. (Source: Wikipedia)